Zoë

A people full of the life and nature of God!

Rudi Louw

The Holy Scriptures are just that, HOLY.

Statements enclosed in brackets were inserted into Scripture quotations to add emphasis or clarify the meaning of what is being said in those scriptures. The integrity of God's Word to man was not compromised in any way. Due care and diligence was cautiously exercised to keep the Word of Truth intact.

For example: The apostle Paul said in his second letter to Timothy in chapter three verse sixteen that:

"All Scripture is given by inspiration of God (literally God breathed)*, and is profitable for doctrine, for reproof, for correction, for instruction **in righteousness**,"* NKJV

Content

The marvel of the
Holy Bible

1. The *theme* and *inspired thought* of Scripture continues *uninterrupted*.

It took *1,500 years* to compile the Holy Bible, involving *more than 40 different authors*, yet the theme and inspired thought of Scripture continues *uninterrupted*, from author to author, from beginning till end.

2. Absence *of mythical stories:*

Compare philosophies and theories about creation in the Middle East, Europe, Asia, Africa and Latin America, and you'll find mythical scenarios, gods feuding and cutting up other gods to form the heavens and the earth. In ancient Greek mythology, the Greeks see Atlas carrying the earth on his shoulders. In India, Hindus believe 8 elephants carry the earth on their backs.

But in contrast, Job, the oldest book in the Holy Bible, declares that *God suspends the earth 'on nothing.' (Job 26:7)*

This was said millennia before Isaac Newton discovered the invisible laws of gravity that delicately balance every planet and sun in its individual circuit.

In contrast to every other ancient attempt to give a creation account, *the Holy Bible pictures the creation of the earth in a very scientific manner.*

In Gen 1 for instance, the continents are lifted from the seas, then vegetation is formed and later, animal life, all reproducing *'according to its own kind,'* **thus recognising the fixed genetic laws.**

Finally, we have the bringing forth of man and woman, *all done by God in a dignified and proper manner, without mythological adornments.*

The rest of the Holy Bible follows suite.

The narratives are **true historical documents**, *faithfully reflecting society and culture,* **as history and archaeology would discover them thousands of years later. Not only is the Holy Bible historically accurate, it is also reliable when it deals with scientific subjects.**

It was not written as a textbook on history, science, mathematics or medicine, *yet, when its writers touch on these subjects,* **they often state facts that scientific advancement would not reveal or even consider until thousands of years later.**

While many have doubted the accuracy of the Holy Bible, time and continued research have consistently demonstrated that the Word of God is better informed than its critics.

3. The Holy Bible is *intact*.

Of all the ancient works of substantial size, *the Holy Bible against all odds and expectations survives intact.*

Compared with other ancient writings, the Holy Bible has more manuscripts as evidence to support it than any ten pieces of classical literature combined!

The plays of William Shakespeare, for instance, were written about four hundred years ago, and written after the invention of the printing press. Many of his original words have been lost in numerous sections, *yet the Holy Bible's uncanny preservation has weathered thousands of years of wars, contradictions, persecutions, fires and invasions.*

*Jewish scribes, **like no other manuscript has ever been preserved**, preserved the Holy Bible's Old Covenant text through centuries. **They kept tabs on every letter, syllable, word and paragraph**.*

*They continued from generation to generation to appoint and train special classes of men within their culture **whose sole duty it was to preserve and transmit these documents <u>with perfect accuracy and fidelity</u>**.*

Who ever bothered to count the letters, syllables, or words of Plato, Aristotle or Seneca for that matter?

When it comes to the New Testament, the actual number of preserved manuscripts is so great that it becomes overwhelming.

There are more than 5,680 Greek manuscripts, more than 10,000 Latin Vulgate manuscripts and at least 9,300 other versions; there exist a further 25,000 manuscript copies of portions of the New Testament.

No other document of antiquity even begins to approach such numbers.

The closest in comparison is Homer's <u>Iliad</u> with only 643 manuscripts. The first complete work of Homer only dates back to the 13th century.

4. In dealing with time, the Holy Bible *accurately foretells what will happen ahead of time, with unmatched results*.

No other ancient work even begins to attempt this.

Other books claim divine inspiration, such as the Koran, the Book of Mormon, and parts of the Veda.

But none of these books contains predictive foretelling.

This one fact we know for certain, and it is undeniable: *While microscopic scrutiny would show up the imperfections, blemishes and defects of any work of man, it magnifies the beauties and perfection of God, just as every flower displays in accurate detail, the reflection and perfection of beauty, so does the Word of Truth when it is scrutinized.*

Historian, Philip Schaff wrote:

'*...Without money and weapons, Jesus the Christ conquered more millions, than Alexander, Caesar, Mohammed and Napoleon.*

Without science and learning, He (Jesus the Christ) shed more light on things human and divine than all philosophers and scholars combined.

Without the eloquence of schools, He (Jesus the Christ) spoke such words of life as was never spoken before or since and produced effects, which lie beyond the reach of orator or poet.

*Without writing a single line, He (Jesus the Christ) set more pens in motion, and furnished themes for more sermons, orations, discussions, learned volumes, works of art, and songs of praise, **than the whole army of great men of ancient and modern times combined.**'* (The person of Christ, p33. 1913)

Today, there are literally billions of Bibles in more than 2,000 languages,

...*isn't it about time you find out what it really has to say?*

Hey listen, the Holy Bible is all about Jesus, the Messiah, the Christ,

...*and everything about Jesus Christ is really about YOU!!*

Study Tips:

Read 2Corinthians 5:14, 16, 18, 19, and 21.

In the light of these Scriptures it should be obvious that if you want to study the Holy Bible,

…you should study it in the light of mankind's Redemption!

Daily feed on Redemption Realities, found in the book of Acts, Romans 1 through 8, Ephesians, Colossians, Galatians, 1Peter 1, 2Peter 1, James 1, 1 and 2Corinthians.

Acknowledgement

I want to acknowledge and thank one of my mentors in the faith, Francois du Toit, for blessing and impacting my life with revelation knowledge.

The portion on *"The marvel of the Holy Bible"* was borrowed from his website: http://www.mirrorword.net/ as students so often feel they have a right to do with things that come from teachers they respect. Just as Galatians 6:6 says: *"Let him who is taught the Word **share in all good things** with him who teaches."*

A special thank you goes to Vanessa Mills Cappucci for first preaching this message way back in 1987 and impacting my life with these truths!

To all our dear friends and family, and to all those who have helped me with this project,

…but especially to my wife Carmen:

For all the love and support,

THANK YOU!

Foreword

Thank you for taking the time to read this book.

Let me start off by saying that *I am totally addicted to my Daddy's love for me;*

…I am in love with Jesus Christ, *and that is enough for me!*

The love of God is so much more than a doctrine, a philosophy, or a theory; it is so much more and goes so much deeper than knowledge; *it way surpasses knowledge,*

…we are talking heart language here,

…therefore this book was not written to impress intellectuals with knowledge and philosophy, theologians with theories and doctrine, nor English majors with grammar and spelling for that matter,

…so if you come up with any other definitions or find any language inaccuracies please don't use it to disqualify Love's own message I bring to you in this book.

I write *to impact people's hearts;*

...to make them see the mysteries that has been hidden in Father God's heart, concerning Christ Jesus, and really *concerning THEM,* so as to arrest their conscience with it, *that I may introduce them to their original design, and to their true selves;* **and present them to themselves perfect in Christ Jesus,**

*...and set them apart unto Him **in love,*** as a chaste virgin,

We are involved with the biggest romance of the ages;

...therefore this book cannot be read as you would a novel; *casually.* It is not a cleverly devised little myth or fable.

It contains revelation and *truth* into some things you may or may not have considered before. It is not blasphemy or error though.

It is the TRUTH of God, ultimate TRUTH, and therefore has direct bearing upon YOUR life, **the Word and the Spirit is my witness *to the reality of these things!***

Be like the people of Berea the apostle Paul ministered to in Acts 17:11. Open yourself up to study the revelation contained in this book, *to see if these things are **true and real**.*

*...but be forewarned, do not become guilty of the sins of the Pharisees, **or you too will miss***

out on the depth of fulfillment God Himself, who is LOVE, wants to give you.

(Jesus said of the Pharisees and Sadducees that they strain out every little gnat BUT swallow whole camels. What He meant by that is that *some people seem to have it all together when it comes to doctrine and they love to argue.*

It makes them feel important, but it is nothing other than EMPTY religious and intellectual pride.

*They know the Scriptures in and out, and YET they are still so IGNORANT about **REAL TRUTH that is only found in LOVE;***

*…they are still so ignorant and indifferent **towards the things that REALLY MATTERS.***

They are always arguing over the use of *every little jot and tittle* and over the meaning and interpretation of *every word of Scripture.*

The exact thing they accuse everyone else of doing though; the precise thing they judge everyone else for, *they are actually doing themselves,* that is: **they often completely misinterpret and twist what is being said, *making a big deal of insignificant things,***

…while obscuring or weakening God's real truth; the truth of His LOVE

*They are always majoring on minors, **because they do not understand the heart of God***

*…**and therefore they constantly miss the whole point of the message**.)*

Paul himself said it so beautifully:

*"…the letter kills but **the Spirit BRINGS LIFE**;"*

*"…knowledge puffs up, but **LOVE EDIFIES**."*

I say again:

Allow yourself to get caught up in the revelation I am about to share.

Open yourself up to study the insight contained in this book *not only with a desire to gain knowledge, but also with anticipation **to hear from Father God yourself**;*

*…**to encounter Him through His Word**;*

*…**and to embrace truth, in order to know and believe the LOVE God has for you**,*

*…so that you may get so caught up in it, **that you too may receive from Him; LOVES' impartation of LIFE***

*If you take heed to these things, and yield yourself fully to it, **it is custom designed and guaranteed to forever alter and enrich your life!***

"In Him was life (zoë)

and that life (zoë) was the light
of men,

and the light shines in the
darkness,
and the darkness could not
comprehend it."

"That was the true light (…that
zoë) which gives light to every
man who comes into the world."

"Although no one took notice of Him, He was no stranger to the world; He always was there and is Himself the author of all things.

It was not as though He arrived on a foreign planet;

He came to His own,

yet His own did not recognize Him.

Everyone who realizes their association in Him,

convinced that He is their original life and that His name defines them,

in them He endorses the fact that they are indeed His offspring; begotten of Him.

He sanctions the legitimacy of their sonship.

These are they who discover their genesis in God beyond their natural conception!

Man began in God.

We are not the invention of our parents!"

- John 1:4, 5, 9
(10-13 The Mirror Bible)

Prayer

Father I just thank and praise You, Lord God,

…that we are found in Your presence,

…and as we focus together on Your truth,

…the truth of our design and our redemption,

…I thank you that we are schooled by Your Spirit, Father,

…Your Spirit of Truth,

…and each and every one of us gets possessed by Your Spirit, Father God,

…by Your supernatural truth and power, my Father,

…as we wrap Your word around our hearts and get caught up in Your love!

I thank you right now, that as our spiritual ears are inclined, our spiritual eyes are being forced wide open, *to see as we aught to see,*

…and to stand equipped by the Spirit of God,

…to go out and be what we are made to be,

...and to do what we are called to do!

I thank you my God,

In Jesus' almighty name!

Be glorified in our midst as we share together in this book, my God!

We worship You Lord!

Amen

Chapter 1

The strong desire for fellowship with the divine nature!

If there is one thing God wants every one of His children that correctly understand His grace message to get, it is that every morning as we spend time in His presence, *we are being schooled in the presence of God;*

…we are getting schooled in the presence of God for service;

…to go out into darkness and shine as we are called to shine!

I am so aware of the fact that as I am sitting here writing I am sitting in Heaven's presence **now**,

…in Truth's eternal presence,

…in God's eternal presence,

…**I am caught up in eternity**,

…and as you are sitting here right now reading this, you too are getting caught up in heavenly places now; *in God's eternal presence.*

But you see people all around you, the people of this world, *are caught up in a season of life,* whatever season of life they may be in, *but* **they are caught up in that season**,

…and their entire mentality in life is **to earn wages and to spend the wages**,

…to earn wages, *to live from hand to mouth the whole time,*

But we who know God's grace in truth, *we have discovered our lives,*

…we have found ourselves!

*…we have **found** our lives,*

…our lives are hidden with Christ in God!

And we, **we are possessed by the Spirit of God!**

Even as I am writing this, I want to tell you, *I really am possessed by the Spirit of God,*

…and overwhelmed right now,

…because the word I want to bring you is from God, **it is so from the heart of God!**

So I want you to open your heart and receive what God wants to give you in this book!

It is His pure word that we speak,

…it is a mature word I am writing; *I am writing in the very presence and sight of God,* amen!

What I want to be sharing with you on in this book is: *the SUKAY (PSUCHE) nature, versus the ZOE nature, the nature of God.*

…that SUKAY life, versus the ZOE life of God.

The word SUKAY **refers to the span of a human life, the season that man lives on this earth. It refers to your natural life, your natural existence**,

*…*like when Jesus said in Matthew 6:25,

"Don't be anxious, (or don't get nervous) *about your life,* (your SUKAY)*"*

The ZOE nature, or the ZOE life, **refers to the life of God, to eternal life.**

You know, as I was studying my Bible yesterday, I realized that when the fall of Man came and he became separated from that ZOE, that life of God he was designed for; *that eternal life,*

…at the same time also, an intense desire was born within his heart.

You see, because of what Man was designed for, because he was designed for it, within Man's heart, within his nature, within his spirit-nature,

…deep within the core of every human being, from our very origin, from even before the Fall,

…but especially since the fall of Man, throughout the ages, we have had an intense desire to have fellowship with that divine nature.

…that is then what gave birth to religion, as well.

You see, religion, fallen Man's effort to try and connect to the divine nature, is as old as mankind itself.

But religion, however, sincere as it may be, remains just a good attempt at best, a sincere guess, *but it still falls short!*

So, Man is by nature religious, and was born with an intense desire to have fellowship with the divine nature, even if he has settled for alternative fulfillment in the mean time, his own heart, the core of his being is still longing and crying out for what he was designed for!

Thus, throughout the ages we have had an intense desire to have fellowship with the divine nature,

…and you see, *with God it is the same thing,*

Before the creation of the earth *that exact same desire* is then also the desire that motivated God to create the earth in the first place!

It's the bringing forth from Himself that divine nature; *His very own image and likeness* that motivated Him to make Man.

And so when He created mankind, He created us to sow forth His glory, *to multiply the divine nature,*

…because we are His image and likeness, amen (Genesis 1:26 & 27)

That's why He said to Adam in verse 28,

"Go forth and multiply, fill the earth"

Why?

Because within Adam was that eternal life, *the life and nature of God, that divine nature.*

I want you to take a mental note right here, underline it or write it down for yourself or something, but let it sink down into your spirit that,

…ZOE life is the life of God; it's the life and nature of God which is eternal life.

It is full of eternal life!

…*it is what eternal life is!*

29

So, ZOE life is the life of God with eternal life in it,

ZOE is the life and nature of God which is eternal life,

...but really __*it's enjoying a quality life with God.*__

That's what that eternal life is, amen!

...*enjoying the life and nature of God!*

...*enjoying the life of God with Him!*

Now when God created a body for Adam, and then made Adam, *He made him with this nature.*

There is a nature that He placed within Adam and He said:

"*Go forth and multiply, and fill the earth with it!*"

He created and made Adam from Himself, and brought him forth,

...*with the divine nature already inside of him,*

...*because He brought him forth from within Himself; from Himself,*

He made him with this nature that He placed inside of him and He said:

"Be fruitful and multiply, and fill the earth with that glory inside you; with My glory!"

"Fill the earth with the divine nature; with the life and nature of God,"

"Fill it with eternal life!"

God said to Adam,

"Go forth and multiply,"

…**because with the life and nature of God within you, you can only show forth the glory of God,**

…*and you can only <u>sow</u> forth the glory of God, amen!*

Ha… ha… ha…

It just goes forth naturally, amen!

But when the Fall of Man came in, what happened?

Adam became a new creation.

He became a partaker of the Satanic nature, and the nature of God became suppressed, it went dormant within him.

Evil was breathed into his mind and into his soul and into his spirit. It was a foreign nature, a new nature to Adam.

He received that evil nature into his nature.

He received the nature and the life of evil.

And what happened then was, we could say that the entire earth began to sow forth the life and nature of Satan,

Humanity began to sow forth the glory of Satan.

And that's why God, as soon as He saw it and knew what happened, He testified, and declared over and over again throughout ancient history,

He said,

"As surely as I live, the earth shall be filled and covered with My glory ...and not the glory of Satan!"

That prophetic declaration started right there in the beginning, right after the Fall happened, before Adam and Eve even left the Garden,

God said, Genesis 3:15,

"And I will put enmity between you (Satan) *and the woman, between your seed and her*

Seed; you will bruise His heel, but He will crush your head!"

And so God interceded and instituted His divine plan.

What did He do?

The entire earth now was part of the glory of Satan,

…it was covered with the glory of Satan.

The entire earth was thrown into utter darkness,

…it was covered in darkness,

…because what happened was that when Adam fell, he became sense ruled,

…and when you are sense ruled, *you are ruled by your five natural senses, sight, smell, taste, touch and hearing.*

…and this is what happened to the entire world, to all of humanity!

The dominion of darkness *talked about in the Scriptures* **is referring to the senses.**

Now what happened is that **God had to come and invade the sense realm, *and give birth to His own nature again.***

I want us to see what actually happened through the gift of Christ Jesus!

Through the gift of Christ Jesus, what did God have to do?

He basically invaded the sense realm of the human being.

He invaded the sense realm,

…and His Spirit moved upon a woman,

…and the seed of the word she embraced and believed, the incorruptible Seed of God was planted within her,

…because, the entire sense realm now, the entire sense realm, was in utter corruption.

The ZOE life had fallen away *or gone almost completely dormant*

And what happened to Man as a result?

Man now only lived for a season,

…everything was now only for a season and totally tied to seasons,

…whereas before, everything was created for all of eternity, to live in a glorious eternity, and to be totally connected to eternity,

…but now everything was made subject to corruption, everything was now sown in corruption,

…and mankind would now only live for a season of life.

But what God did, He desired to birth His nature again, to sow forth His glory on the face of the earth again,

…so what He did was, His Spirit came upon and hovered over and moved upon a women named Mary, and God placed the seed of His word, and through it His incorruptible Seed, within her life, and she gave birth to a son, Jesus Christ.

And Jesus totally invaded the sense realm.

He walked within the sense realm.

I want you to see clearly that when Jesus walked, He walked within the sense realm, *but yet He still walked within a different realm,*

…**He walked in the realm of faith,**

…*whereas the entire earth was ruled by their senses.*

People, we need to see this,

…we need to see how the entire earth was sense ruled, *they were ruled by their senses,* and they lived from moment to moment. Satan had them gloriously trapped,

*…gloriously trapped **in living from day to day,***

…until he was thriving!

I tell you, he was thriving, *because the glory of his nature was spreading throughout the whole earth,*

…but I am telling you **that was not the plan of God!**

We read in Psalm 33:11

"But the Lord's plans stand firm forever; His intentions can never be shaken"
                                                    - New Living Translation

The English Standard Version says,

"The counsel of the Lord stands forever, the plans of His heart span to all generations.*"*

In Isaiah 46:10 God says,

"I make known the end from the beginning, from ancient times, what is still to come. I say, 'My purpose will stand, and I will do all that I please!"   - New International Version

The Revised Standard Version puts it this way in that last part there:

*"…**My counsel shall stand, and I will accomplish all my purpose**"*

He goes on to say in verse 11,

*"**I have spoken and I will bring it to pass; I have purposed, and I will do it**."*

Verse 12 & 13,

*"**Hearken to Me, you stubborn of heart, you who are far from deliverance: I bring near my deliverance, it is not far off, and My salvation will not tarry; I will put salvation in Zion** (My enlightened people) **for Israel** (all my people) **are my glory!**"*

And so we see how God had birthed His son.

He invaded the natural realm, the soulish realm, the sense realm, the (PSUCHE) SUKAY realm, the natural life.

He invaded it with His ZOE, with His life!

*…**with His image and likeness, with His divine life and nature!***

He invaded the sense realm, the SUKAY realm, the natural life realm *with His eternal life!*

He invaded the SUKAY *with the ZOE.*

And so what happened was that Jesus started walking in this SUKAY realm, in this natural life realm, in this sense ruled realm, *but He walked by faith, He walked in another realm of life, ZOE life, eternal life, AGAPE life, God's own life of love,*

…and what happened was, the world did not understand, they could not comprehend this LIFE, they could not comprehend this LOVE,

…because the love which was in the SUKAY realm was PHILAO love,

PHILAO **is the kind of love born of a human being**

…it is the kind of love born of being a human.

In other words, **it is a life that is a love of a human life;**

…it's the human being's love for being a human.

In short, **it's the natural love of a human being,**

…it's a sense realm love,

…a sense ruled love,

It's the love born of the senses.

...born of the SUKAY realm.

It is the love of a human life.

That love is centered around Self.

It is centered on Self.

'I love you the way you are; I love the way you look, I love him for who he is, but if you love someone else, I'll kill you!'

But you see the AGAPE of God; the LOVE of God is a love of a different kind, *of a different origin.*

It is born out of ZOE, out of the divine nature, out of the nature and life of God that is within us.

It's a love to where I'll lay down my life.

'I will lay down my life for my brother.'

That is ZOE life; that is AGAPE love!

That is why when Jesus walked on the face of this earth, *they could not comprehend the life and love in which He walked.*

They could not comprehend it, *because they had no understanding of it!*

You see, Jesus walked *in that realm of faith,*

...whereas the entire world, even His own disciples were ruled by the senses.

They were ruled by the senses and by sense knowledge,

...that's why they could not comprehend many of the things which He said,

...until after the resurrection and their eyes were opened, *and they received and embraced that new nature; the ZOE nature of God.*

It was not a new nature, amen, *but it was new to them,* amen.

Sense knowledge has to do with the way you interpret life

...because of what you are able to perceive and learn through the sense realm, by your senses only,

...and by what you have experienced in this life,

...this natural life,

...this sense dimension life,

...this SUKAY life!

Chapter 2

God placed His seed within us!

Okay, now I would like to take you with me to John chapter one.

John 1:4

"In Him was life (zoë)*"*

So as he walked upon the earth, in Him was life, in Him was the ZOE nature.

"In Him was life (zoë) *and that life* (zoë) *was the light of men"*

Now why was His life …why was *this life* (this zoë) the light of men?

Because the senses in which they were trapped in, the senses which they were walking in, *was utter darkness,*

…and when they saw the ZOE life of God manifested in their midst <u>it became a light</u>,

…and that is why we see that the multitudes always followed Jesus Christ,

…because of the ZOE nature,

He did not keep it bottled up within Himself, inside Himself, but He released it.

And I am telling you that as surely as you are reading this book His glory shall cover the earth,

...but you see that glory, the glory of God shall not cover the earth <u>until each and every one of us fully embrace and release the ZOE nature which God has placed within us; inside of us.</u>

...until every one of us so fully embrace these things as to step out boldly and say,

'Father I'm releasing the ZOE nature that you've placed within me!'

And so what it goes on to say here in John 1 is,

Verse 5,

"...and the light shines in the darkness (in the senses, in the sense realm, where people, even His disciples are trapped, living in the natural dimension of life) *and the darkness could not comprehend it,* (and yet could not ignore it, or put it out and make it go away either)"

In 1Corinthinas 2:14 it says that,

"The natural man (the SUKAY ruled man) *does not comprehend the things of the*

spirit realm, of the Spirit of God, because they are foolishness to him."

So, getting back to the people in Jesus' day, *they could not comprehend this life and this nature that Jesus Christ manifested in their midst.*

Verse 10 to 13 says,

"He was in the world, and the world was made through Him and the world did not know Him. He came to His own. His own did not receive Him, but as many as received Him, to them He gave the enlightenment and thereby the right to again become, (or to again exhibit the fact that they are) *the children of God."*

He clarifies and says that He is talking to the whole world and including every person in this conversation, and in this work of redemption, he says,

"...to them He gave the right to become (or to exhibit again the fact that they are) *the children of God"*

"...even to those who believe in His name, who are born not of blood, nor of the flesh, nor of the will of Man, but of God"

I love the way these verses are translated in the Mirror Bible,

John 1:10-13

"Although no one took notice of Him, He was no stranger to the world; He always was there and is Himself the author of all things."

"It was not as though He arrived on a foreign planet; He came to His own, yet His own did not recognize Him"

(Psalm 24:1, *"The earth is the Lord's and the fullness thereof, the world and those who dwell in it [RSV]."*

The word *"recognize"* **paralambano**, comes from **para**, a preposition indicating close proximity, a thing proceeding from a sphere of influence, with a suggestion of union of place of residence, to have sprung from its author and giver, originating from, denoting the point from which an action originates, intimate connection; and **lambano**, to comprehend, grasp, to identify with)

"Everyone who realizes their association in Him, convinced that He is their original life and that His name defines them, in them he endorses the fact that they are indeed His offspring, begotten of Him; He sanctions the legitimacy of their sonship."

(The word often translated, *"to receive,"* **lambano**, means to comprehend, grasp, to identify with.

This word suggests that even though He came to His own, there are those who do not grasp their true origin revealed in Him, and like the many Pharisees they behave like children of a foreign father, the father of lies [John 8:44].

Neither God's legitimate fatherhood of Man nor His ownership is in question; *Man's indifference to his true design is the problem.*

This is what the Gospel addresses with utmost clarity in the person of Jesus Christ.

Jesus has come to introduce Man to himself again; humanity has forgotten what manner of man he is by design! [James 1:24, Deuteronomy 32:18, Psalm 22:27].

The word *"begotten"* **genesthai** [aorist tense] is like a snapshot taken of an event,

…from **ginomai**, to become, to be made, to be birthed, or brought forth [see John 1:3].

The **Logos** is the source; *everything commences in Him.*

He remains the exclusive Parent reference to their genesis.

There is nothing original, except the Word!

Man began in God [see also Acts 17:28].

"He has come to give us understanding to know Him who is true and to realize that we are in Him who is true" [1John 5:20].)

The words *"endorses"* and *"sanctions"* **exousia** is often translated *"power;"* as in, He endorses, or He sanctions, He gives power to become (or **to be brought forth**) children of God.

It is a compound word. **ek**, always denoting origin or source, and **eimi**, I am; thus, **out of I am!**

This gives legitimacy or *"endorsement"* and authority or *"sanction"* to our sonship; our **teknon**, translated as offspring, or child.

"...to them He has given" **didomi**, in this case to give to someone that which already belongs to them; thus, to return.

The fact that they already are His own, born from above, they have their beginning **ginomai** and their **genesthai** their very being in Him, that fact is now confirmed in their realizing of it!

Convinced, **pisteo**; His name **onoma**, defines Man [see Ephesians 3:15]. *"He made to be their true selves, their child-of-God selves."* - The Message Bible says)

"These are they who discover their genesis in God beyond their natural conception!

Man began in God.

We are not the invention of our parents!"

I am telling you that when the Spirit of God comes upon us, just like the Spirit of God moved upon Mary,

…when the Spirit of Truth comes upon us and He hovers over our lives and moves upon us as we read and understand the Scriptures and comprehend what God is saying, *we find ourselves in exactly the same scenario as what happened with Mary when He placed His seed within her.*

The exact same thing happens to us, *within our spirit and within our lives,*

God places His incorruptible seed within us, within our hearts and within our lives.

I can still remember how it happened in my life.

I was just sitting there listening to the word; I was listening intently to what was being said because I was hungry for truth, and as I was still sitting there absorbing it and taking it in, the Spirit of God began to move upon me, and He began to strongly convict and persuade me of sin, righteousness and judgment,

…as I began to comprehend that Jesus was wounded for my transgressions, that He was bruised for my iniquities, that my sin was laid upon Him, and that I was justified and made righteous there in His death, and in His resurrection, and that the devil was defeated there, *that truth began to judge Satan's lies in me, and I became free in my inner man,*

…and I felt like I was getting born again, starting totally over, born anew, everything suddenly became fresh and clean *as the incorruptible seed of God's truth was placed inside of me, within my heart, and came to life there!*

You see that day, *faith was born in me; faith was given birth to in my spirit!*

You see we are born anew **of an incorruptible truth; of an incorruptible seed;**

…and an incorruptible nature is awakened within us,

…it is the life and nature of God that lay dormant within us,

…but it now germinates and comes alive and gets born again, it comes to life;

…it is born afresh and anew through the embrace of truth!

That water of the word *awakened within me that dormant life and nature of God, the divine nature;*

…*that original image and likeness of God in which I have always been made!*

48

And now, just like Mary gave birth to a son, Jesus Christ,

...just like with Mary, *we give birth to a new life, to that new child within us, we give birth to our sonship, to the life of Christ, to Christ within us!*

...we give birth to Christ; we give birth to the Christ-life!

That's exactly what Paul talked about when He said that **Christ within you is the hope of glory!**

It is God's hope of His glory restored within you and upon the earth!

So we are born anew by the incorruptible truth of the Gospel and by the incorruptible seed of God watered and awakened within us.

God places the seed of His word, of His truth within you; *He places His seed within you, and that seed connects with the seed already within you,*

...even as you are reading this book,

...and there is an impartation, and a comprehension, and a conception within the womb of your understanding, and within the womb of your inner man, of your spirit, and you become born anew.

So we are born again and brought forth again, as sons of God, of an incorruptible nature,

...the incorruptible nature of God within a life of corruption!

I want you to realize that you are not of this earth!

You are born of the incorruptible seed of God's nature!

Even where the entire word around you is living in corruption, **you can fully exhibit and give clear expression to the life and nature, the ZOE of God within you,**

...you can fully give expression to that eternal, abundant quality of life you enjoy within your bosom!

We are sustained, **that expression within our lives are sustained *by the incorruptible seed of God's Word, of God's truth, of God's Gospel,***

...whereas the entire world around us is living in corruption, they are living in a season of life, in a span of life called SUKAY

...**but every one of us who embrace God's Gospel,** *have stepped out of life, out of that SUKAY,* ***into a realm of eternity,***

...we have stepped out of life, out of that death, ***into life, into ZOE, into eternal life!***

Now what does it mean to receive eternal life, to receive the life of God, to receive that ZOE life of God?

It means that you sit out; *you no longer participate with this world in their corruption.*

It means you step out; *you are no longer trapped in a world ruled by the senses.*

Chapter 3

We must manifest the ZOE life of God!

I want us to see it so clearly that people in this sense realm in this SUKAY realm, they are running around just like it says, somewhere in the Scriptures,

…they are flying from continent to continent, *looking for fulfillment, looking for meaning in life, looking for truth, looking for that glory they don't have, **looking again for what they have lost track of but which is inside them already.***

They are empty and they are looking for that ZOE life, *for the life of their original design,*

…but they can't find it anywhere,

…until the light of the Gospel comes into their life and shines upon them,

*…**until the truth of the Gospel dawns upon them …upon their hearts and upon their understanding!***

That hearts cry within Man, that heart and passion within Man, **that strong desire after the divine nature** *to again fellowship and interact with that divine nature* **is the most important, most outstanding feature in a man's life!**

It's the thing that stands out the most when you look at humanity!

Listen, we who get the truth, we who grasp it, *we are indebted to live in the Spirit,*

…to release the ZOE life which God has placed in us, and awakened in us,

…to release it to mankind,

…because, if we aren't doing that, **then we are keeping God as a prisoner within our lives,**

…we are keeping His ZOE life locked up within us,

…and worse yet, the rest of mankind is condemned to eternal death.

Romans 10:14 & 15

"But how are men to identify with and relate to Him in whom they have not believed?"

"And how are they to believe in Him of whom they have never heard?"

"And how are they to hear without a messenger or an accurate representative?"

"And how are men to reveal and proclaim this Gospel, unless they realize that they are sent to do so?"

"For it is written, 'How beautiful on the mountains are the feet of those who proclaim and reveal the Good News!'"

In John 10:10-15 Jesus is sharing, and He is telling the people why He has come, He says:

"The thief (speaking of Satan) *comes only to steal and kill and destroy;* (BUT) *I came that they* (those stolen from and destroyed by Satan, really, all of mankind, amen,) *...I came that they may have life* (zoë), *and have it* (zoë) *more abundantly"*

"I am the good (genuine, truthful) *shepherd. The good* (the real) *shepherd* (who loves the sheep) *lays down his life for the sheep."*

...that ZOE life makes us good shepherds also, amen,

"He who is a hireling (or a fake) *and not a shepherd, whose own the sheep are not,* (...that sounds like Cain to me, *'...am I my brother's keeper?'*) *...he sees the wolf coming* (...the devourer, the SUKAY life, the devil in disguise) *and he leaves the sheep*

and flees; and the wolf snatches them and scatters them."

Verse 13,

"**He flees because he is a hireling and cares nothing for the sheep**."

"**I am the good** (true) **shepherd; I know My own, and My own know Me, as the Father knows Me, and as I know the Father; and** (they know Me as) **I lay down My life for the sheep**."

So, **we who have embraced the truth of the gospel,** *we step out of the SUKAY nature, and we are of course no longer in the senses,*

…we are no longer caught up in a hum drum day to day routine,

…but **we step into the reality of eternal life,**

…and day and night has no more meaning for us,

…there is no time there in that eternal realm,

*…***no more time-bondage-thinking!**

Someone told me last week,

'I lost my watch recently and I don't care, I'm living in eternity!'

Ha… ha… ha… we don't need to get that crazy, amen,

…**but we do have to realize that we are eternal beings,**

…that the spirit realm, that realm of eternity, that that ZOE life realm **is more real** *than this natural world, than SUKAY life,*

*…****and we do have to start seeing everything from that perspective, amen!****

There is no time in this realm we live in, in this realm of LIFE;

…in this ZOE realm **time serves us,** *not the other way around.*

Time does not exist in this realm.

Paul put it this way,

*"****For me to live is Christ****, and to die is gain!"*

He said,

*"****My life in the flesh means only one thing to me now, <u>fruitful labor</u>!****"*

When He said,

*"****Redeem the time…****"*

What he meant was,

"Let redemption (the work of redemption; Christ's work of salvation) *have its perfect work,* (allow it to impact time, allow it to impact your time, allow it to guide and steer your life, allow it to impact and influence and change the world, this natural SUKAY life!)"

He meant,

"Make the most of every opportunity!"

Hey, don't allow the devil to try and trip you *to fall back into the mindset of the SUKAY nature!*

He wants nothing more than to trap you *in that mindset!*

Don't allow it!

Through understanding and believing the gospel, *you have become intertwined with the ZOE nature of God!*

...you have stepped into a new realm of life!

...a new realm of God's life, where you are walking and manifesting the nature of God, amen!

2Peter 1:2-4 says it this way,

"Grace and peace will be multiplied to you (in the gospel) *in the knowledge of God and of Jesus our Lord."*

He says,

"God's divine power has granted to us all things necessary for life and godliness, (through the gospel) *through the knowledge of Him* (who called us out of darkness into His marvelous light; into His marvelous LIFE)

…*who called us to* (enjoy and exhibit) *His own glory and excellence of LIFE* (…the excellence of His ZOE),

…*by which* (by His own glory and excellence, and through the gospel) *He has granted to us His precious and very great promises* (…the promises of salvation and of being able to partake of God's eternal ZOE life)

…*that through these* (through these promises, through the gospel, through the knowledge of Him, through partaking of those great redemption realities and gospel truth), *through these you may escape the corruption that is in the world through lust* (…through strong but rather empty, misguided, ill-conceived, and ill-begotten, destructive desires,) *and become partakers of the divine nature."*

He says,

"…through these (…through the knowledge of Him, through the gospel, through partaking of eternal truth and redemption realities) *you become partakers of the divine nature!"*

Now why did God in His desire to spread His glory across the earth have to come through the vehicle of Jesus Christ?

Because Jesus, from before the beginning,

(…and also in being human Himself, having taken on and partaken of flesh and blood,)

…He Jesus fully represents the whole human race, *in order that He might become the first born among many brethren!* (Romans 8:29)

And let me tell you, just as it says there in Romans 8:29, *we were jointly formed in the image of His Son,*

…and therefore we, as His brethren, are not of an inferior nature to Jesus Christ!

We are walking in exactly the same nature, the same quality of nature, manifesting the life quality of God, the ZOE of God to mankind, amen!

That is the truth about us!

So let's embrace it fully, amen, *and live it!*

Chapter 4

Eternal LIFE!

So, we see why Jesus came to earth, **He came to give us life (ZOE),** *He came to give us that ZOE life more abundantly!*

…He came to multiply that which was in His life!

…He came to multiply the incorruptible seed!

…the incorruptible seed of God's word, the incorruptible seed of God's life!

John 12:24

"Unless a grain of wheat falls into the ground and dies, it remains alone, but if it dies, it produces much grain!"

…of the same quality and of the same kind, amen,

…the kernel of wheat in the harvest precisely or exactly matches the grain of wheat that was sown,

…and fell into the ground, and died!

Turn with me quickly also in your Bible to
1Peter 1:23-25

*"**You having been born anew, not of
corruptible** (perishable) **seed, but of
incorruptible imperishable seed, through
the living and abiding word of God,** (through
the truth of God, through the gospel);"*

*"…**because all flesh is like grass, and all its
glory, like the flowers of the field. The grass
withers, and the flowers wilt and fall to the
ground, but the word of the Lord** (the truth of
God, the truth of the gospel,) **abides forever!**"*

*"**This word is the gospel, the Good News
which was preached to you!**"*

Here you can clearly see how there is the
SUKAY life, contrasted by the ZOE life of God!

The SUKAY life is compared to the grass of the
field.

As beautiful as the flowers of the fields are, so
the glory of the flesh is also beautiful, *for a
moment …but it will fade in its beauty,*

*…it starts to wilt and wither away and it ends
up falling to the ground,*

…disappointing you again!

But as we take a hold of the truth of the gospel,
I am telling you, *we take a hold of eternal life;*

...we are intertwined with the incorruptible, imperishable seed and ZOE of God,

...the eternal life and nature of God!

...incorruptible and imperishable!

...eternal truth, eternal life, eternal ZOE, amen!

Through the gospel, through believing the gospel, we have taken ahold; we have intertwined with a glorious God, *who is love,*

*...*and we are manifesting His life and His love nature to a lost world!

I am telling you, we are manifesting His life, *a life that is flowing straight through our very being,* to a lost and dying world, amen!

This is also something that I want you to realize: **Because of the fact that we have been born out of the same incorruptible seed as Jesus,** *God is holding each and every one of us responsible to do what Jesus did,*

...to lay a hold of His word of truth,

...to lay a hold of our spirit identity,

...to lay a hold of our true identity,

...**to walk in a sensitive relationship to that Sprit of truth,** *that is within us, that we have from God,*

...and therefore to walk as Jesus walked!

Why is God holding us responsible *to do what Jesus did and to walk as Jesus walked?*

Because we have been born of that same incorruptible imperishable seed that God placed in Mary's womb, *that is the same incorruptible seed we have been born from,*

...that same incorruptible imperishable seed as Jesus,

...**and we are kept in that perpetual state of living in that victory, and living in that life and nature of God, living in that Zoe, in that same life,** *by the same incorruptible seed of truth,*

...**that imperishable word of truth;** *the gospel of our creation and of our origin and of our salvation in Jesus!*

And so I am telling you that **if we do not walk as Jesus walked on the face of this earth,**

...then we are insulting the word of God, we are insulting the word of His grace, we are insulting the gospel,

...and we are insulting the intelligent truth about us!

...we are insulting God's intelligence and our own!

I want you to know and realize that within us is a full potential!

...within us is the full potential to walk just as Jesus walked!

Our embrace of the gospel gives us access to that!

Our embrace of the truth gives us access to that!

Faith gives us full access to it all!

Peter says very clearly there in 2Peter 1:1 that we,

"...have obtained a faith of equal standing with the faith of the apostles,

...in the righteousness of our God and Savior Jesus Christ!"

Paul adds his full agreement and amen to that when he said in Romans 5:2 that,

"...through Him, we have obtained access by faith into this grace in which we stand!"

He goes on to say,

*"...and we now rejoice in the living hope
and full expectation of fully partaking of
and sharing in the glory and ZOE life of God*

*...and we now also rejoice in the fact and
expectation of that glory of God now being
manifested through us!"*

**Within us is the full potential to walk just as
Jesus walked!**

...to walk and minister in that nature!

...to walk and manifest that nature!

If we can just see and take notes on how Jesus
walked on the face of this earth,

**He walked in absolute authority over every
other authority, *over every other expression
of life that was contrary to the ZOE life of
God, and that would manifest around Him!***

**He walked in absolute authority over every
demon of hell!**

They recognized His personal mind!

They recognized His spirit!

They recognized who He was in His person!

They recognized Him personally!

66

They recognized His authority!

And I'm telling you what Jesus had in His spirit *we can have in our spirit, as well!*

We can have that same mind!

Why?

Because what Jesus had in His spirit *we HAVE in our spirit as well, already, amen!*

And that is why God is now holding us responsible to walk *in acknowledgement of what is within us,*

He is holding us responsible to walk *in acknowledgement of what we have in our spirit!*

He is holding us responsible to walk *in acknowledgement of who we are!*

Let me tell you, the truth is, *we are not of this earth!*

And until the Church, until the believers, until we, the body of Jesus Christ, **starts walking in the reality that, *'I am not of this earth,'*** we are going to remain defeated, *and we are not going to fulfill the purpose of God!*

I am telling you, when I walk up and down in my room, in my private time of prayer, sometimes I say,

'Father, I am not of this earth! I am here for one reason. I am here to demonstrate the power and glory of God in this darkness all around me! I am here to shine forth!'

Just as it says there in Philippians 2:13,

"For it is God who works in you both to will and do of His good pleasure"

Paul goes on to say there in Philippians 14-16

"Do all things without murmuring and disputing, (…without arguing with God about the truth of the gospel, and rebelling against Him, refusing to live that truth)

"Do all things without murmuring and disputing, so that you might become blameless and innocent and harmless,

…children of God without fault, in the midst of a crooked and perverse generation, among whom you stand out and shine as lights in this world, <u>holding fast the word of life</u>!"

"…so that I may be comforted and excited about the fact that I did not run in vain all over the known world, and labored in vain among you with the gospel!"

Let me tell you that that light of the gospel, and that light that is within you, *is not of an inferior quality!*

The gospel is not of an inferior quality!

It is the very power of God at work in us who believe!

That light, that life; that ZOE, that is within us is not of an inferior quality, of a lesser quality *than the life, than the ZOE that Jesus walked in!*

It is that exact same quality of life!

It is that exact same truth of the gospel!

...that exact same truth of the word of God!

...of the very LOGOS that came out of Heaven,

It's the very ZOE life and AGAPE love nature of God that is within us!

It's the very image and likeness of God we were made in!

The quality of life Jesus enjoyed and walked in came from the LOGOS!

The LOGOS was His very substance!

Both Jesus and we came from the same LOGOS!

That light, that life; that ZOE, that is within us is not of an inferior quality, of a lesser quality *than the life, than the ZOE that Jesus walked in!*

...**and we are shining forth that quality of life in the midst of a crooked and perverse generation!**

...***walking just like Jesus walked!***

In John 17 Jesus prays for the disciples, *and for us who would believe in His name through them,*

...and He prays, and he says,

Verse 9,

"***I pray for them,*** *I am not praying for the world* (...because they are still caught up in darkness and running after SUKAY life) ...***but I am praying for those whom You have given Me*** (Those who have believed and embraced the truth of the gospel). ***They are Yours; all Mine are Yours, and Yours is Mine. I am glorified in them.***"

Let me tell you, ***Jesus Christ is glorified in our lives!***

Hallelujah!

Glory to God forevermore!

"...***and all Mine are Yours, and Yours is Mine! I am glorified in them.***"

John 17:11,

"And now I am no longer in the world..."

Jesus was talking about the reality that He was leaving the world and going back to His Father.

"...but these are in the world, and I come to You holy Father, keep through Your name

(...through Your word, through Your truth, through that identification with You, through their identification with You, keep) *those whom You have given Me, that they may be one as We are one!"*

Let me tell you something, *we are one!*

This whole notion that people are praying for and praying towards, *praying that we might become one,*

...and gathering together trying to promote unity,

...praying and promoting unity and oneness in the SUKAY minded realm *is going to fail,*

...it's going to fall apart every time!

Because we are already one!

It's a reality in the ZOE minded realm!

...in the spirit realm!

It's a reality already, *for those who can grasp it and see it through the gospel <u>and embrace it as reality</u>!*

...they are the ones who experience unity and oneness and peace!

It's a oneness we enjoy already *in the truth of the gospel,*

...but it's not a SUKAY realm oneness,

...it's a oneness we enjoy in the ZOE realm!

You see when we, *through the gospel,* **begin to all receive of, and partake of the ZOE nature of God and *we become ZOE minded,***

...and not SUKAY minded;

...we enter into that realm of reality,

...that oneness and unity becomes reality to us!

You see in reality we are all partakers of the ZOE nature of God,

...but we have got to become ZOE minded,

...we've got to become eternity minded,

...and we have got to become internally minded, *God living inside me minded,*

...and we've got to walk in the reality that <u>we are not of this earth</u>,

'I have found my life; my life is hidden with Christ in God!'

*...*we've got to understand and start walking **in the reality** that, *'I am left on this earth **for one purpose,***

*...**for one purpose,***

*...*and that purpose is: **To manifest the nature of God and to invade the realm of the senses!'**

We are called to be invaders of the realm of the senses!

We are called to walk in that same realm that Jesus Christ walked in!

We are called to walk in the realm of AGAPE love!

God forbid that there be any strife left in the body *after we have received and embraced this revelation!*

Let me tell you that **if you walk ZOE minded,**

*...**then you can only walk in the AGAPE love of God!***

And let me tell you that **as we walk in that realm of love,** *that is how and why the world will know that we are all one,* **them included,**

...it is because we are walking in love, and we truly love one another, and we truly love the people living in this world.

That's the only reason why the world will take note of these things,

...and how the world will also discover these things to be truth and reality for themselves as well!

I am telling you that **in the embrace of the truth of the gospel,** *we are walking in the realm of faith <u>to where we are not of this earth</u>,*

...but we discover that we are as foreigners, we are aliens, and we are like sojourners on this planet.

That may be a nice little cliché to some, ***but it's a reality!***

It may sound like a nice little cliché, but I am telling you, ***we are not of this earth!***

We are not born of the will of the flesh!

We are more than flesh and blood!

We are not born of the will of Man!

We are not mere men!

We are spirit beings!

We are born form above!

We are born of God!

In the fleshly life, in the SUKAY life you may be born of this earth,

…but in the spirit, in your spirit, you have not been born of this earth!

"And now we are indebted to walk after the spirit and not after the flesh!" - Romans 8:12

Okay, let's get back to John 17, and let's read again there from verse 11,

"And now I am no longer in the world, but these are in the world. And I come to you holy Father, keep through Your name those You have given Me, that they may be one as We are one!"

So, we see that in the ZOE mind, that, *we are one,*

…and as we see that from the ZOE mind,

…*then we are ONE!*

"While I was with them in the world, I kept them through Your name, those whom You

gave Me I have kept, and none of them was lost, except the son of perdition (the rebellious son)"

Okay verse 13,

"But now I am coming to You, <u>and these things I speak to them</u> in the world,

...that they may have My joy fulfilled in themselves!"

Verse 14 says,

"I have given them Your word; and the world has hated them <u>because they are not of the world, even as I am not of the world</u>."

Okay, so there He Himself states very clearly *that we are not of this world!*

We are in this world, *but we are not of this world!*

"I do not pray that You should take them out of this world, but that You should keep them from the evil one."

"They are not of this world, even as I am not of this world!"

There He finds it important and necessary to repeat Himself!

Chapter 5

God's purpose for our lives

Now listen to me very carefully.

What happened when you embraced the gospel and began to realize that you too are a partaker of the eternal nature of God?

You welcomed and embraced the expression of that ZOE nature through you!

You embraced the manifestation and the exhibition of that ZOE nature in your life!

Now throughout the ages it has been God's desire to have fellowship with that divine nature *that is within you,*

…it has been His entire reason for creation, to have fellowship with the Devine nature inside of Man, *inside each and every one of us,*

*"…**that they may be one with Us, and with one another, as We are one!**"* as it says there in John 17:11 we just read.

…and now that you have tapped into that ZOE nature, **you have yielded to the purpose of God for your life** *and for this planet!*

I am telling you it does not please the Father to have Satan put sickness upon mankind, it does not please Him.

It does not please the Father to allow that stuff to be put upon **His own dear children,** *and He will do anything to get us out of the hands of the tempter, and the deceiver, and the destroyer, the wolf!*

That is not His plan for us!

So why doesn't He just take us out of this world when we embrace the truth of the gospel?

Because of His intense love for lost humanity!

It is because of His intense love for lost humanity that He has left us on the face of this earth!

Jesus said,

"My food is to do the will of the One who sent Me!"

"As the Father has sent Me, <u>so send I You</u>!"

And so now we can stand with Him and say,

'*Father, my food is to do the will of the One who left me here on this earth*'

He has left us on this earth **because of His intense love for confused humanity who has lost their way!**

...and really He didn't leave us; He didn't me here all alone, He is right here with me, amen!

I want you to really know it deep down in your spirit that just because we are in this earthen vessel for a season,

...just because we are walking in a real world out there, *does not mean it can hinder us from having fellowship with the divine nature that's in God!*

It is not able to hinder God from having fellowship with His divine nature that He has placed inside of us!

God has desired that fellowship throughout the ages!

Because of the curse, we have all been caught up in the mentality, that one day when we get to Heaven, then suddenly we are going to stand in the presence of God, *and we are all going to become angels,*

...but it is absolute nonsense. I know; I also thought that way.

I used to think that, one day when I'm dead, **then** *I will finally arrive,*

…just like I heard someone once say: *'After death, then comes perfection,'*

…but I am telling you *it is absolute rubbish!*

And this whole world we live in, that's what they walk in, *that is what they are thinking,* **that's the wrong understanding that they have.**

They think that when death or yet another resurrection comes there is going to be a mighty transformation and transfiguration within their spirit, soul and body,

…but I have news for them, **if you have embraced the seed of God, the word of truth,** ***the gospel of your salvation in Christ's work of redemption,***

…**and the incorruptible life,** ***the imperishable ZOE life and nature of God has been awakened in you,***

…***then there is nothing left to be changed or transformed,***

…even when Jesus comes back again, just like He promised that He would, **what is mortal is going to get swallowed up by life (ZOE),**

…***it is going to get swallowed up by what is immortal!***

…***by that which is already within you!***

*All that will remain will be **what is already immortal,***

*…**a glorified body!***

*…**a spirit body!***

*…**in every way equal to the body Jesus has now,***

*…**in every way equal to Jesus' spirit body!***

John says in 1John 3:2

*"**Beloved, we are children of God now; it does not yet appear what we shall be like, but we know that when He appears we shall be like Him, for we shall see Him as He really is.***"

And then verse 3 says,

*"**And everyone who thus hopes in Him purifies himself as He is pure!***"

He says, chapter 2 verse 28,

*"**And now, little children, abide in Him, so that when He appears we may have confidence and not shrink from Him in shame at His coming.***"

And that is why it is so vital for us **to get awakened in our inner man,** *for us to get awakened unto our righteousness,*

*...**for that ZOE life to get awakened within us,** and not to get caught up in that SUKAY mentality!*

I want you to see that **there is no eternal life; there is no ZOE life <u>outside of God</u>,**

...there is no partaking of ZOE life outside of embracing the gospel and embracing Jesus and embracing the Father, embracing His living Spirit within you!

That same apostle John says in 1John 2:23 & 25,

*"**No one who denies the Son has the Father.**

He who confesses the Son (...who comes in agreement with whom the Son is, and with what the Son did for him in the work of redemption,) **he has the Father also**."*

*"**Let that which you have heard about,**

...that word that concerns your beginning,

...let that abide in you.

...If what you heard about that, about your beginning, about your true origin, where you really come from,

...if it abides in you, <u>then you will abide in the Son and in the Father</u>.

...And this is what He has promised us, ZOE life; eternal life!"

1John 5:11 &12,

"And this is God's testimony which He has borne concerning His Son, Jesus Christ,

...that God gave us eternal life,

God gave us His ZOE, His life and His nature,

...and this life, this ZOE is revealed and awakened in His Son.

...He who has the Son, in other words, he who believes the Son's message, the gospel, he who believes in the Son's work of redemption and embraces it and embraces the Son, has life,

...he has that ZOE life,

...it is awakened in him;

...he who has not the Son of God has not the life, has not the ZOE life awakened in him."

He says in verse 13,

"I write this to you who BELIEVE in the name of the Son of God,

…that you may know you have eternal life,

…that you may know you have that ZOE life inside of you!"

Verse 20 says,

"And we know that the Son of God has come,

…and He has given us understanding

…to know Him who is true,

…and to know that we are in Him who is true,

…in His Son Jesus Christ!

…This is the true God, and eternal life, that ZOE life!"

John says in 1John 2:6-8

"He who says he abides in Him, ought to walk in the same way in which He walked."

He says,

"Beloved, I am writing you no new commandment, no new truth in other words, but I am writing to you about the truth that is as old as time, older than time really, I am writing to you about the oldest of commandments, the oldest of words

84

spoken by God, which you have heard about, which concerns that which was from the beginning, your origin in God an your original design in His image and likeness."

Verse 8,

"I am writing to you as if it is fresh, as if it is a new word, as if it is a new commandment,

...and this thing is concerning what is true in Him <u>and in you</u>,

...because the darkness is passing away and the true light is already shining!"

Hallelujah!

He says, verse 17,

"And the world is passing away and the lust of it;

...but he who does the will of God abides forever!"

Again a reference to ZOE life, or eternal life, versus SUKAY life, or life in the natural, a fleshly soulish life,

...which is abiding in death, *abiding in separation from ZOE,*

...living in separation from the life of God inside you,

…in separation from God Himself,

…in separation from life itself!

So I say again, do not get caught up in that SUKAY mentality, in the snare of the enemy, as we have seen with practically the entire religious so called Christian Church of the Lord Jesus Christ, *they are almost totally useless, like they have no sense!*

And why do they have no sense?

Because they are walking around with the full power and potential of God within their spirit,

…and yet they do not know it, *because they have refused to believe it and acknowledge it!*

They'd rather believe a lie and agree with the lies of the enemy and with deception, *because they tolerate a measure of darkness still in their lives,*

…because they prefer darkness to light!

…they prefer to believe a lie over the truth!

The battle was won over 2014 years ago now; *the devil was utterly defeated,*

…*the lie was exposed and the truth was revealed,*

...the light has already come to enlighten their spirit, and there is enough power available for them to walk totally totally free and in absolute authority over a defeated foe,

...but they refuse to enter in behind the veil that was rent over 2014 years ago!

The way has been opened; the place has been prepared,

...Jesus says, *"I've gone to prepare a place for you,"*

...the life, the ZOE has been made available and given access to,

...but those who associate themselves with Jesus, who are supposed to be believers, *have been walking in the mentality of a SUKAY world,*

...they are walking in the mentality of a sense ruled world and have refused to embrace God's faith, *that's why they have not been living and walking in victory and in these things prepared for them.*

1 John 5:4,

"Whatever is born of God overcomes the world;

...and this is the victory that overcomes the world, faith,

...God's faith in us!"

Verse 5 says,

"Who is it that overcomes the world, but he who BELIEVES!"

And that faith, that word of faith, that revelation of God's faith, that revelation of God and of us, *which God came and revealed Himself in Jesus and in the work of redemption,* <u>**that faith does not ignore or make light of what God has revealed!**</u>

Paul says in Romans 10: 6-8

*"**The righteousness based on faith says, 'Do not say in your heart, 'Who will ascend in to heaven?'** (...that is, to bring Christ down from above again to fix what He already fixed, as if He never came)* **or 'Who will descend into the abyss?'** *(...that is, to bring Christ up from the dead, as if He is still down there, as if His work was a failure and He was never raised from the dead as proof of the success of redemption.)*

*...**But what does this faith say? What does the faith of God say to us?***

*...**That faith speaks a clear word to us, and it says, 'The Word, the truth, is near you, in***

your heart and on your lips (*…that is, the word of faith, that word of God's faith, that word of truth, God's version of what the truth is, that word of God's gospel concerning our redemption in Christ Jesus, which we preach),"* he says.

For centuries now religious Christianity, the Christian religion, the so called Church of the Lord Jesus Christ has been walking in the same mentality as the SUKAY world, as the sense ruled world, *and that is why they have not been able to show forth the glory of God's grace,*

…they have not been able to show forth, or sow forth, the real glory of God!

…they have not been able to show forth, or sow forth, the glory of His nature and His love for mankind!

It is theirs; it is already in them, they have everything necessary to exhibit it and reveal it and impart it and awaken their fellow man in it,

…*but they have not been mindful of it,*

…they have been blinded in their understanding; they walk in a darkened understanding, *and they are not ZOE minded, eternity minded, internal life and eternal life minded!*

But God desires for them to wake up out of sleep **and see these things clearly** so they too can say,

'Father, I know why I'm on this earth. I know why You have left me here on this earth and didn't take me home the moment I believed on Jesus and received Him as my Savior. I know why You have blessed me to be here; I am here to invade the sense realm!'

'And Farther there is an urgency that is now given birth to in my spirit, because I've realized that I've discovered that treasure the whole world is looking for, I've found it, My life is hidden with Christ in God, that is the greatest treasure worth everything. The greatest treasure to enjoy! I've gained eternal life, I reach for it, I reach towards that upward call to fully lay a hold of all that Christ has come to reveal to me and has laid a hold of me for. I've tapped into the ZOE life of God, into the life and nature of God, the very glory of God, the glory we all were designed for but fell from in the Garden! I've laid a hold of it!'

'Father and if there is one thing I now desire, it is to pull down every work of darkness that comes across my path! I desire to join You and go around destroying every destructive work of the evil one!'

Even those who have seen these things have not fully believed it *and therefore they are not speaking out in boldness and releasing this!*

...because as a man thinks in his heart, as a man believes about himself, so is he!
- Proverbs 23:7

The whole world is crying out for the coming forth, and the stepping out of the sons of God, the manifestation in fullness of the glory of God within the sons of God, *but as long as the children of God remain sense ruled they are going to be of no use here on planet earth!*

There is an old saying and a lying deception that has been around for years and it says:

'You are so heavenly minded that you are of no earthly use!'

But hey listen, **become so heavenly minded that you are totally of earthly use, of earthly good, practically in your life, amen!**

At one time I got so caught up in the gospel, in the grace and love of God, I got so caught up in God, and I still am that way, but I was so excited and lost in my Father's goodness, so caught up in that heavenly realm that one of my brothers accused me of having my head in the clouds.

…He said, you are floating around here, oblivious to what is going on around you; your feet aren't even on the ground, come back down to earth and get a life man, you won't be able to get or keep a job the way you are carrying on.

Ha… ha… ha… it really bothered me when he said that, and I started thinking, *'you know, maybe I should dial it down a bit, maybe I should stop caring about others so much, maybe I should scale back my zeal and enthusiasm a bit,'*

…but you see I was so in love with my God, and wanted others to see the truth of the gospel so much that I didn't quite know how to do such a thing, *and really I didn't want to!*

And as I was still praying about this and asking the Lord about it, some lady in a Church meeting I was attending somewhere handed me a little prophetic word of encouragement she had written down for me on a piece of paper.

This is what God had to say through her:

'My Son, become so totally heavenly minded that you become an absolute fanatic for God, for I want to make you a revolutionary fellow, full of truth and love that will bring about a reformation in My Church!'

That word hit me so hard, and made such an impact and a lasting impression on me that I forgot I was a man and started crying like a baby. Ha... ha... ha...

I stopped caring what others think of me, and I still don't!

That word stuck with me all these years and just added more fuel to my fire!

Listen, don't let anyone put out your fire!

Listen that is how each and every one of us have to become, *white hot for God,*

...that is how each and every one of us are going to have to start walking, *as if we are aliens upon the face of the earth,*

...walking in a totally different spirit than the world, *to the point where we are so totally manifesting the glory and the life and the love nature of God, that ZOE life, that others will have to start taking notice.*

It is the only way we are going to get this world *to open their ears to what we have to say **and see what we have to say,***

...and become innocent children of God themselves, blameless and harmless in the midst of this crooked and perverse generation we live among, this crooked and perverse world we live in.

We really are aliens and sojourners, and we are just here to invade and plunder the sense realm,

"...so get ye up into a high mountain, and lift your voice with strength!"

Let's go up to the high places, let's rise up within ourselves, *in God's strength and might, and with His truth,*

*...*and let's lift up our voices with confidence and boldness and strength, and proclaim this gospel of God in clarity, *because that is what we have been called to do, amen!*

Glory to God!

Man, I am telling you; **we are not normal people; we are not just mere men; we are not just normal human beings;**

...**we are a peculiar race, a royal priesthood, a holy nation, God's own special people; God's very own children,** *called out of darkness into His marvelous light,*

...**called out of this world,** *and sent back into this world to make an impact!*

We are God's pleasure!

Our first ministry is always unto God!

And out of that place of intimacy and fellowship with Him *in His truth and in His love <u>we impact this world</u>, amen!*

Now I have had to learn wisdom through the years *in accurately representing and presenting the true gospel,* and living life among normal people,

…I mean, I have had to learn to act normally *and communicate the truth more accurately and clearly,*

…instead of coming across like some religious nut job to people,

…but my passion has never diminished, and I have refused to let anyone rain on my parade,

Ha… ha… ha…

Just like Paul said in 2Corinthians 5:13:

"For if we are beside ourselves, it is for God; if we are in our right mind, it is for you"

Ha… ha… ha…

God has made us able ministers of a New Covenant!

Hallelujah!

He has made us able ministers unto Himself!

As I said before, *no human myth, or circumstance, or opinion of Man,*

…nor the voice of my senses,

…**it is not going to be allowed to hinder my divine fellowship with God, my ministry unto Him daily!**

He has also made us able ministers unto others!

…to where we invest the truth into their lives, *God's truth and love,*

…and to where we minister into their lives and prophecy over their lives, *building up our brethren and our fellow Man,*

…until our fellowship, and our fellow Man, and this body of Christ, *becomes so valuable because we all become ZOE life minded,*

…and we all now together, **we are now all living for one plan, *and giving our lives for one purpose,***

…**we are all now intertwined with the desire and the heart plan of God that He has been working on throughout the ages!**

You see then God becomes so precious,
because we realize that not one of us is of this earth,

...and we are then moving as a body through this sense realm, ***to impact and transform it!***

Chapter 6

You are salt and light!

Let's quickly go to Matthew 5:13

"You are the salt of the earth, but if the salt lose its flavor, how shall it (the earth) **be seasoned? It** (the salt) **is then good for nothing but to be thrown out and be trampled underfoot by men"**

I want you to take this scripture and relate it to the state of the so called Church for the past 2014 years.

2014 years ago the veil has been rent *and a place has been prepared for us,* **so that we may enter,**

   ...through insight and revelation and faith,

   ...into the very presence and bosom and holiness of the Father, and live and abide there,

   ...but for the most part, *the Church has not entered in,*

   ...has not entered into that rest of faith,

...as a result, they have been trampled underfoot by men, and the principalities and powers have mocked the religious Church, they are laughing, and they are throwing it in God's face, saying to Him,

'God when You gave Your Son, you had such faith that mankind would respond properly and appropriately, but look at them, they are just as deceived and weak as they have ever been before, and we still control them; they are just like salt without saltiness, and they are useless, they are good for nothing, they are worthless, except to be tripped up and beaten and trampled underfoot by mankind!'

...and so God has been despised in the world, because the religious Church *has been living in darkness itself **and misrepresenting God,***

...what Paul says of the Jews in Romans 2:24, is true of the religious Church also:

"For it is written as a testimony against you: 'The name of God is blasphemed among the Gentiles because of you!'"

But listen I have news for you and for those principalities and powers, ***God is opening the eyes of those who are hungry for truth***

...and are tired of being defeated and being a punching bag for the devil and for the world,

...and God is raising up a new body of BELIEVERS in this day who have within them the living word of God,

...who are full of the faith of God,

...full the ZOE live and nature of God,

...who see themselves and this whole world the way God sees us,

...and they are manifesting and releasing that truth and that life, that ZOE into the nations,

...and they are challenging the devil in people's minds and thinking and hearts, <u>head on</u>,

...and undoing his power and authority that he wields over them only through deception and lies.

...out of these BELIEVER'S bellies, out of their inner man, out of their spirit they are allowing the Spirit of God to flow,

...they are releasing and allowing the ZOE life and nature of God, and the AGAPE love of God to flow out of them and invade the sense realm, to invade the realms of darkness, to invade the gates of hell and plunder the devil's so called kingdom, his stronghold which he has tried to set up and maintain in the earth.

…but you see the earth does not belong to him, and he has been defeated already,

…and what he thinks he has under his control and influence is being taken away from him by the truth of the gospel and by the ZOE life and nature of God flowing out of those who have BELIEVED the truth of the gospel!

Hallelujah!

The gospel is the power of God unto salvation for everyone who believes it, amen!

Matthew 5:14

"You are the light of the world. A city that is set on a <u>hill</u> and cannot be hidden."

I am telling you the ZOE life and nature cannot be hidden!

For years and years, **because of deception and because of fear,** the religious Church have locked themselves up within their four walls,

…afraid to be contaminated, afraid to get their hands dirty, afraid to go out there and face the world,

…and they have preferred to rather lock themselves up in their closet, *in their prayer closet, and just pray and pray and pray and pray for God to move,* **and they have wasted precious time praying for revival <u>when they are supposed to be the revival everywhere they go</u>!**

I am not saying you should not pray, man don't get me wrong,

…**but pray as you go man, pray as you go, or pray a little until your faith is strengthened and then go,** *but listen, we are called to go, we are not called to sit and wait.*

Wait for what?

The veil has been torn over 2014 years ago now already, *and all the revival you would ever need was released in the resurrection.*

Revival came when the New Creation came and was given birth to in the resurrection.

We have resurrection power flowing on the inside of us already, *because we have been reconnected with the I AM.*

Jesus, who is the resurrection and the life lives in us. The Ever Present One lives in us.

That resurrection power is an ever present reality within us,

...**because the same Spirit that raised Christ from the dead dwells and abides in us permanently!**

And so when you get out there up on that hill, *and you lift up your voice with strength* ***revival will come flowing out of your own heart!***

...and the heavens won't tear open, *because the heavens were already rent and torn open when God invaded the sense realm over 2014 years ago now,* ***and completed our salvation,***

...**and therefore there is still an open heaven over us today!**

It has never been closed, *and that veil can never again be sewn up, and heaven can therefore never be shut back up again,*

...**not as long as our representative is alive and well and seated at the right hand of God!**

Listen there is a man seated in heaven right now, at the right hand of the Father, *and as long as He is sitting there we are sitting there with Him,* ***and have the same access as He does,***

...we have equal access to the throne of grace to receive a breakthrough in the time of need, *when we draw upon heaven's resources* ***by faith,*** *amen!*

We are seated with Him, with Jesus, in that place of authority, *far above all principalities and powers and might and dominion,*

…above every other name or influence that can be named, not only in this age, *but in any and every future age to come, amen!*

"Let your light so shine before men that they may see your good works and glorify your Father in heaven!"

Listen; there is no such thing as being a secret agent for God.

There are no introverts in God's kingdom.

Your faith is not a private matter; *it is a public matter.*

Your faith wasn't given to you, *just to die with you!*

We have all been called to be confident witnesses of the truth of the gospel.

To be His witnesses!

The righteous is as outspoken and bold as a lion, *and nothing shall intimidate them!*

Paul says, *"As it is written, 'We have believed and so we speak,' therefore, we too have believed and therefore speak!"*

But let's get back to Matthew 5:14

"You are the light of the world. A city that is set on a <u>hill</u> and cannot be hidden."

Verse 15,

"Nor do they light a lamp and hide it under a bushel, but set it <u>on a lamp stand</u>, and it gives light to all those who are in the house."

I want you to take a pen or a marker of some sort and do yourself a favor. Underline right there in your own sacred Bible those words *"hill"* and *"lamp stand"*

Verse 16,

"Let your light <u>so</u> shine before men, that they may see your good works,

(…that they may see your life on display, that ZOE life and nature of God your Father, your Daddy and their Daddy) *and give glory to the Father"*

<u>*"Let your light so shine…"*</u>

"In Him was life (zoë) *and <u>that life was the light of men!</u>"*

I am telling you, that life, that ZOE life and nature of God in us is the light of men!

Listen let me repeat myself; **we are not living a closet Christian life.**

We have done that for way too long!

There is a time for the closet, and for prayer, *and my first ministry is always unto God,*

…and in His presence, and in intimate fellowship with Him, **I am equipped and imparted to** *and I receive revelation that revolutionizes my thinking and my heart and my life!*

…**but if we do not receive that divine feedback and communication of God in our spirit,**

…*that divine seed, that ZOE life that is from God, that daily impartation of truth, and the renewing of the mind,*

…**through the washing of the water of the word,** *through the embrace of redemption truth; of eternal truth,*

…*then there can be no Spirit ministry going forth, there can be no life imparted, no ZOE life,*

…because Jesus said,

"My words are spirit and life!"

...and without embracing daily that impartation, that spirit and life, that ZOE life and nature of God there will be no anointing for ministry, and no impact, and no breakthrough in people's lives,

...and then we might as well stay home and go hide in the closet, or under the bed, or in our business, and on the job, and not go out ever again, or speak out ever again, amen!

Listen, it is so important for us to understand this progression, *this development that takes place **and equips us and prepares us for ministry to the world.***

It is so important for us to understand this principle.

Your first ministry is always unto God.

If you do not receive divine feedback form God every day, *then you are on a dead end road, <u>and you need to get your heart and faith right, so you may receive life.</u>*

So your first ministry is unto God, then unto the body of Christ; other fellow believers, your brothers and sisters *who have seen the truth and know themselves to be children of God.*

You see and this fellowship that you have with God automatically releases and blesses your fellowship with the body of Christ,

...it connects you to the body of Christ and adds a definite quality, and enrichment to that fellowship with other believers, with that body of Christ,

...then what happens?

Then there is a perfect prayer and a perfect flow, *and we are moved upon and we move out as a body and from the body, **going forth and plundering the SUKAY realm!***

Plundering it through the ZOE life and nature that is within us, *and for the ZOE life and nature that is within us, amen!*

We the children of God have got to become *dominated by eternal life!*

...otherwise we will be of no earthly use!

...salt that has lost its saltiness!

That salt is referring to the word of God, to the truth of the gospel!

Jesus prayed there in John 17,

"Father, sanctify them by Your truth, Your word is truth!"

We need to get sanctified, *cleansed from the mindset of the world!*

There are still so many followers of Jesus *that are* **totally intertwined** *with the world* **and the thinking of the world** *and the systems of this world.*

…and so every time someone gets sick, there is nothing wrong with going to get medical attention *when you truly need it,* **but people either don't know, or they forget that we have a covenant of healing with God, and instead of standing on the truth of the word and applying that truth through the confession of their faith,** they are filled with fear and quickly run to the doctor for every little thing and to the hospital,

…and they live totally in that natural dimension and give more weight to the word of that doctor, or to the word of that circumstance and symptoms speaking to them, **than they do to the truth of redemption and the word of God.**

…and then what happens if the doctor cannot help them?

They end up dying, needlessly, many of them, prematurely!

…because they live totally defeated lives, double-minded lives,

…running to and fro between the SUKAY and the ZOE,

…they are stuck *and get nowhere in their faith.*

…that kind of faith is futile, and it might as well be in vain,

…because it is totally neutralized by fear and ineffective,

…their faith is non-active, almost non-existent!

But in Jesus that kind of faith was brought to an end!

The time of living that way has come to an end,

…and must come to an end in us!

It is about time, no, it is high time *for the children of God* <u>*to become eternal life dominated!*</u>

When we become eternal life dominated, *then we will find ourselves ruling and reigning as kings in this life!*

…ruling as we are supposed to rule!

Chapter 7

Reigning in life!

Let's also take a look at Romans 5:17

"For if by one man's offence death reigned through the one,

...much more those who receive the abundance of grace and the gift of righteousness will reign in life through the one Christ Jesus!"

The Weymouth Translation of the Bible reads,

"...will reign as kings in this realm of life through Jesus Christ!"

Right now as you are sitting here reading this book, *you are sitting in the presence of God,*

...and God is saying to you: *'You in the body of Christ, YOU will reign in this life!'*

You see individuals have stood up at times. Mighty men and women of God have stood up as individuals, *but that is not the total fulfillment of prophecy,*

...almost all the Old Testament prophecies and the whole of the New Testament *declare a rising up of the body!*

...and I am telling you now, *so you can be included in that body,*

...listen, a body of BELIEVERS is standing up, and rising up,

...*and they are living and ruling and reigning in this life as kings!*

What do kings do?

They rule over a nation!

They rule over whole nations!

...*multiple nations even, some of them!*

They rule within their domain!

They rule over everything within their domain!

Jesus has been given a domain!

And let me tell you, *we have been given a domain together with Jesus,*

...*we are joint heirs!*

...*we are fellow heirs with Him!*

...and we rule over the nations.

That is our domain.

The nations are our domain.

The ends of the earth, *that is the extent of our domain,*

...nothing less, nothing more!

We rule over every principality and power!

They can no longer influence me!

In fact, I have authority over them, *and I break their power in other people's lives.*

They have no more power!

Compared to the power and authority we have, *they have no more power or authority!*

Why?

Because we are seated in heavenly places!

I am seated with Christ Jesus!

I am no longer trapped!

The devil has no more authority or power; it is all a lie, *because it was all based on lies and deception!*

And the truth has come, *and that truth has set me free!*

You see for too long we have all been trapped, just earning our little salaries,

…just like the people who don't know any better and have nothing else to live for,

…running to our little universities and learning this and learning that, training and education our senses,

…being educated just like them *in the SUKAY nature,* **when God wants to give us more than that!**

God wants to take us beyond that realm of life, and birth within us, and within them, *His word of life,*

…and translate us, and them, ***into a realm of life*** *that Man can never get to in his senses;*

…that Man can never by himself give birth to, just being trained and educated in the SUKAY realm.

To many religiously minded Christians, worldly minded Christians *are still just cultivating their sense realm education,*

…they are being trained up, even in their Bible schools, merely in sense realm knowledge,

…but thank God, He is raising up a body of people, BELIEVERS, there are many of them now *who are cultivating and developing their spirit through truth, real spiritual truth,* not just any old kind of spiritual truths, **but through God's truth, the truth of the gospel, the truth of our original design and identity and purpose,** *and through the truth of our redemption and reconciliation back to the Father, to our Daddy God,* **and back to everything we fell from in the garden and fell short of from the beginning!**

God is raising up a body of BELIEVERS *whose entire attention and spirit focus is on their spirit,*

…and they are cultivating and developing the spirit-life, that ZOE life and nature within them,

…and they are stepping out in boldness, and they are allowing that life, that ZOE life to flow freely!

Let's go to another scripture there in Romans. Romans 12:2

"And do not be fashioned to this world"

"Do not be conformed to this world"

Now Paul would never have written that to Roman believers if that was not a problem in their case.

They lived in Rome, the seat of culture and fashion in those days, the very empire that set the pace in knowledge and development in their day,

...and they were conforming to; they were being fashioned and molded to the world they lived in, and they were being ruled by the SUKAY realm.

They had all the ZOE life of God available to them and within their reach, *it was right there, within them, within their spirit, fully theirs to enjoy,* but they were being ruled by the SUKAY life.

And so Paul says here,

"Do not be conformed, do not be ruled, do not be fashioned by, do not intertwine with the senses, do not become intertwined with the SUKAY realm,

...but rather become intertwined with the living word of God, with the truth as God has revealed it and restored it in Christ Jesus!"

"Be ye transformed by the renewing of your mind!"

Renewing your mind to what?

To that eternal life *reality!*

Being transformed into what?

Into whom you already are *from the perspective of the truth,* not from the perspective of the natural.

...renewing your mind and being conformed to that ZOE life <u>reality</u>, *to the reality of the life and nature of God inside you.*

Allow yourself to be transformed by that reality *into being a living breathing manifestation of the glory of God, of the ZOE life and nature of God,* here on this planet, <u>here in this life</u>!

Being renewed by the truth *in your whole way of thinking,* he says,

...to where you become so intertwined with God, to where you think God's thoughts, and speak God's words, and sing God's songs, *and every step you take is in God,*

...*because you are now engrafted through faith, by the word, you are now engrafted in Christ Jesus.*

From the root of Jesse, out of the most ancient of roots actually, *out of the very LOGOS itself, out of the heart and logic of God, out of His love that was from the beginning,* there came a stem, and that stem was Jesus, **and at the age of 33 that stem was cut off, *and now we have been engrafted in that same root!***

119

And that age 33 refers to a maturity of age; it refers to a mature man, to mature manhood, *it speaks of the maturity of that root.*

And we have been engrafted into maturity, into mature manhood, into the mature nature of Jesus Christ!

We are engrafted into Christ Jesus, into the Father Himself, into His very Spirit and into His very heart and life!

And that engrafting is such a <u>reality</u>,

...it is such a <u>reality</u>!

...it is such a <u>reality</u> that we have been engrafted into!

When Adam was sleeping and Eve was taken out of him and brought forth out of him that was a picture, *a prophetic picture of when Jesus descended into hell for 3 days and 3 nights and the New Creation was created there,*

...it was created out of Him and brought forth out of there, out of that grave, out of that death; ***it was brought forth out of Him and given life to in the resurrection!***

When Jesus descended into the lower parts, into hell itself, and into death and the grave, *he did not descend there into that realm as a defeated being,*

…no, He descended into that realm *as already being a conqueror,* **as being an overcomer,**

…He already lived an overcomer's life, He already became victorious, **and so the New Creation was created out of an overcomer,**

…the New Creation was drawn out of a victor,

…the New Creation was birthed out of someone who was more than a conqueror!

He is more than a conqueror, *and that is the nature that you have been created out of!*

I am telling you man, *hey,* **receive what God has to say to you!**

God is speaking straight into your life today.

He is speaking to you straight out of this book you are reading!

He is speaking straight into your spirit!

He is telling you that you are not just an ordinary person!

We are not just ordinary people; *we are not mere men!*

…and so, reducing ourselves to again pray for the supernatural, *as if it is not ours already, is not right.*

Praying for the supernatural is not right, why?

Because the very fact that we, *the ZOE people of God,* are here in the sense realm,

…it means that *the power of God, and the supernatural, that the very ZOE,* is already also in the natural.

The fact that the ZOE is in the natural realm, in the sense realm, *that is supernatural.*

That is already supernatural!

The supernatural are already here!

I am telling you the supernatural are within us!

The supernatural is already here in the natural, *because the ZOE is already here!*

Where the ZOE is *is the supernatural!*

The very fact that we are walking in a realm of supernatural AGAPE love, and a realm of supernatural faith, the FAITH of God, *is supernatural.*

That is why it is the most normal thing for us, for you, *to expect the supernatural.*

*...**to expect the supernatural in every word you speak into someone's life,***

*...**in every faith step you take** upon the face of this earth!*

*...in every faith song you sing, **do not expect less than a supernatural encounter,***

*...**do not expect less than that supernatural realm to manifest,***

*...**do not expect less than the supernatural!***

I tell you! *Expect it,* **amen!**

Because if we are indebted to live in the spirit, *then we are indebted to live in the supernatural,* *and we can no longer afford to live in this natural life only.*

*We can no longer afford to live in this natural realm life, **but we are to live <u>in a different mentality</u>!***

<u>We are living in a different mentality</u>; we have already reached the highest heights, and we are soaring as an eagle!

Glory to God!

And praise God if we never touch the earth again, *that will be okay by me,*

Ha...ha... ha...

Praise God if we never touch the earth, *because we will never be able to stand upon the earth and lift men up **that way,***

…but we are soaring, and we are drawing them up into heavenly places with us, into the kingdom of the Son of His love!

Romans 12:2

"Do not be conformed, or fashioned after this world, but be transformed, by the renewing of your mind"

You see there is a labor left to be done;

…we are resting in God, *but there remains yet a striving and a labor for us, a price to be paid,*

What is that price?

It is to enter into *and to remain undistracted,*

…caught up in His love and in His rest!

There is a price to pay *to remain there in that place of life and victory, caught up in Him, resting in His love!*

Many people think that now because they have the nature of God within them *that they are automatically now on this water slide, on this super-tube to life in the heavenly places.*

Listen my dear, you are not just going to wash out on the shores of heaven, and there you are, you have arrived.

Hey listen *there is an exertion of energy,*

…an exertion of every effort that has got to come from each and every one of our lives,

…a straining of every nerve,

*…**we have to press into these things** as Paul said to Timothy,*

*"…**make every effort, be diligent to show yourself approved unto God, rightly dividing the word of truth, be a worker that does not need to be ashamed, rightly dividing the word of truth! Lay a hold of eternal life to which you were called, lay ahold of it!***

…laying a hold of your inheritance in God, fully laying a hold of it!"

You see in ministry *this is the price that has to be paid* as he is speaking about in Isaiah 55:1,

*"**Ho, everyone who thirsts, come to the waters; and he who has no money, come, buy and eat! Come, buy wine and milk without money, and without price**,"*

How can you buy without money and without price?

What is that price that has to be paid?

It is the setting aside of your time!

It is the abiding in His truth and in His presence!

It is purposely renewing your mind!

It is cultivating your faith!

...abiding in the faith of God!

But it's not a burden, *because it is a matter of the heart.*

It is a matter of what you treasure;

...it is a matter of being in love.

When you are in love it is not hard. *It is not too difficult.*

There is still a cost, *but you are trading in your old life, <u>for a new life</u>,*

*...like trading in an old worn out broken down Volkswagen Beatle **for a brand new BMW.***

Jesus said,

"My yoke is easy and My burden is light!"

The price comes in, when you don't feel like it, *but you get into it anyway,*

126

*…I mean, when you least feel like ministering to people, **you still go and you do it anyway!***

It's an exertion of your *every effort!*

It's a renewing of your mind, *a taking captive of every thought, and a straightening out of your thinking, and a taking control, and a washing and renewing of your mind <u>by the truth you already know</u>.*

Paul said this also, he said,

"I buffet my body, lest after I have preached to others, I myself become disqualified!"

Sometimes there is a physical price to pay *in traveling and in going out of your way in ministering to others, **a love sacrifice***

*…to where you become a living sacrifice, **being willing,** and making yourself available, **yielding to that ZOE and to that spirit within you, to the spirit of life and to the spirit of love and to the Spirit of God!***

You see; it takes effort sometimes to get to the top of the mountain, *but when I get there, I see everything with a new eye; **I see everything from above, from a new perspective.***

That is sometimes the very process involved in the renewing of the mind also; *there is a time thing to it as well,*

...taking the time,

...making every effort!

There is effort involved, *exerting my spirit and mental energy.*

You see *it does take time to renew your mind.*

You can't renew your mind, *but it takes time spent in the presence of God and in the truth,*

...saying, *'Holy Spirit teach me, open my eyes, I am hungry to know the truth of your word!'*

...and then you take the time, *meditating upon that truth, and pondering upon it, musing on it, thinking about it, and allowing the Holy Spirit to enlighten you, and impart it into your spirit through revelation knowledge,*

...giving you revelation on a much deeper level than just being educated with knowledge in your mind!

You are already complete in Christ Jesus; you are already perfect in the spirit realm, *but the saving of your soul comes through the renewing of your mind!*

"What will it profit a man if he gains the whole world but loose his own soul"

You see that is the price to be paid, *the necessary price* **for the saving of your soul!**

God wants you to have *a saved soul,* **saved all the way,**

...liberated and freed by the embrace of accurate truth, spirit dimension truth, in your inner being!

Jesus said,

"You shall know the truth and the truth shall set you free!"

And when that happens to you, *then you see everything through God's eyes,*

...you see everything through the eyes of love,

...you see everything through your Daddy's eyes!

Hey, I tell you, *we are supernatural;*

...we are walking *in the supernatural;*

...the supernatural is all around us *and within us!*

We are supernatural!

We walk in that reality!

And our purpose is to draw everyone else out of darkness also, *into the kingdom of light,*

...into the light of life, *into the kingdom of God's Son and of His love!*

Chapter 8

Engrafted into Him!

I am so aware of the fact that as we fellowship together around these things in this book, my writing this, and your reading it, **we are communing together in the very presence of God,**

…and we are being schooled together by God, **and we are being equipped in our spirit to go out and face this world,**

*…***to go out and to be used by God as His mouthpiece!**

As I am writing I am so aware of the fact that *it is not me communicating these things to you, into your spirit,* **but it is God Himself who is speaking to you, and imparting to you,** *and God is saying to you right now,*

*'***I am giving you My word, and you are not to be ashamed of My Gospel, because it is filled with power, with My power, it is the very power, all you need, to change and transform every human being on the face of this earth, from the inside out.***'*

'So, you are not to be ashamed of My word in your mouth, of My gospel being communicated in clarity through you, for in it is the very necessary creative power to transform every person's life whom you come in contact with!'

Listen God says,

'Do not allow for any mumbling and grumbling, the language of confusion and unbelief, the argumentative language of the accuser of the brethren, to come out of your friend's lives, even the strangers around you, amen,'

'Listen, you grab them and arrest them by the Spirit, in their speech, right where they are, and you start speaking into their lives, you start speaking truth, the truth of the gospel, and you start prophesying in line with that truth into their heart and life!'

'Because you see, My child, within that word, within that truth that you speak and communicate with them, there is a creative power, the very creative power of God, My creative power, to get rid of that irritable stupid contrary argument and lying deception that is being entertained in the body of Christ, and in the minds of those who live around you!'

So, *when you open your mouth and you dare to speak up,* hold this prayer and thought in your heart,

'Father, I am not ashamed of Your Gospel, for it is Your very power to transform the life of every human being I come in contact with!'

God wants us to develop an urgency in our spirit, *because we know the life that we have within us,*

…and therefore when we go out into the world, and we purpose to speak for the Father, and to speak for Jesus, and to speak for the Gospel,

…there is an urgency in our spirit, because we have found our lives, our lives have taken on an abundant quality, we enjoy abundant life, we enjoy ZOE life; our lives are hidden with Christ in God,

…but there is a certain and definite urgency within our spirit, because we also know that all around us people are running around searching, barely scraping by,

…or running in the rat race of life, earning wages, and trying to amass a fortune, trying to add value and worth to their empty lives,

…but they are getting nowhere in seeking for abundant life,

...even traveling from continent to continent, from vacation spot to vacation spot, they are trying to look for life outside themselves, trying to look for ZOE somewhere out there,

*...**not realizing it is within their reach,***

...not knowing that they need to look elsewhere, other than where they are looking for it,

*...not knowing that what they are looking for is found **in that invisible spirit realm,***

*...it is found **within their very own spirit.***

*Listen as you grasp the gospel **a definite urgency in your spirit is awakened,***

...because you grasp the fact that all flesh is as grass, and all its glory like the flower of the field, no matter how beautiful, eventually it will fade,

*...**but we will not fade because the word of God has come into our lives,***

*...**the breath of God has blown upon us and within us,***

*...**and that truth of the gospel within our lives will stand forever!***

That word of truth that is from above is eternal, *it will stand forever!*

Let's take a look at 2Corinthins, and I am still talking about that root, that mature root, *about the fact of us having been grafted back in again, in Christ Jesus,* **in that work of redemption,**

…we are being grafted into that mature root, through faith

…we, us, **we were grafted into that same maturity,**

…and now as we see it, by revelation, we are also now being grafted into the full expression of that maturity, amen!

2Corinthins 5:17

"Therefore if any man be in Christ Jesus he is a new creation, the old things have passed away, BEHOLD now in Christ Jesus all things have become new!"

Listen let me tell you, when you are standing before God in His presence, and you're ministering unto Him, **He doesn't see you as that worthless old good for nothing person you see yourself as,**

…no, He sees you as you really are, His workmanship, created in Christ Jesus to be embraced by His love.

He created you for the expression of that love and for good works. He ordained you

135

for it from before time began, so you may now walk in it!

God sees only the nature of Christ Jesus on exhibition in you, *because the old you died on that cross, was crucified with Christ and went down into hell,*

...and you, the true you, was raised up in Christ to newness of life!

Your true identity, you, was raised up to newness of life; *you were raised up in resurrection power!*

So when you're standing in God's presence, you are standing there, *already engrafted in Christ Jesus,*

...because 1Corinthinas 1:30 & 31 says,

"Of God are you in Christ! He is the source of your life in Christ. God made Him our wisdom, our righteousness and our sanctification and our redemption,

...therefore it is written 'If anyone wants to boast, or brag, let him not brag on himself, but rather, let him boast in the Lord!'"

So when you stand before God, minister unto Him *from that persuasion, amen!*

Minister unto God *from that cup full of revelation!*

136

"You prepare a table before me in the presence of my enemies; You anoint my head with oil, my cup runs over!"

- Psalm 23:5

And that is not an excuse!

You are walking in resurrection power!

Every stride, every step you are taking, *you are in Him; in Him you are living and moving and have your being!*

We have no other life apart from the life of Jesus Christ, amen;

His life is your life!

I say again; **you do not have any other life outside of that reality!**

That is reality, amen; His life is your life!

Hey listen, and that is not being narrow minded, amen, *that is being broad minded, **life more abundantly minded!***

Ha... ha... ha...

You have to become narrow minded in order to enter into a broad place, in order to enter into eternal life, amen!

...in order to enter into that broad place of life more abundantly, enjoying eternal life!

137

David says in Psalm 16:6,

"The boundary lines have fallen for me in pleasant places; surely I have a delightful inheritance!"

In Him, we live and move and have our being.

In Him we breathe,

...we breathe Him, we live Him, the very songs we sing are Him, the words we speak are Him, everything we do is in Him, there is nothing about our lives that are outside of Him, that is not touched and influenced by the reality of Him.

He is our life!

His life is our life!

His ZOE is our life!

He has made us so totally heavenly minded that we are absolutely of earthly use!

Heaven and earth has become intertwined in us!

We can no longer separate what is heavenly from what is earthly!

Our life here on earth is both sacred and down to earth, both Human and divine!

We can no longer live a dual life, a double standard life, one sacred and one secular.

The life we now live in the flesh is the life of Christ, the very ZOE life of God!

We were, and we are, *engrafted in Christ Jesus,*

…and that life we now live in this flesh and blood body, in the flesh realm, we live by the faith of the Son of God,

…that life we now live, we live by the One who loves us and gave Himself up for us, that we might be reconciled to our Father God,

…and enjoy that ZOE, that eternal life, that abundant living, our original design,

…enjoying it with Him!

Chapter 9

Greater is He that is in you!

Let's look at 1John 4:4 also.

*"**You are of God little children, and you have overcome them** (The world and all the powers of darkness, the SUKAY thinking, the natural mindset) **because greater is He that is in you, than he that is in the world!**"*

This is such a powerful scripture, but it has been made light of, or, even if it hasn't been made light of, *it has not been received in its entirety and in the fullness of what it declares!*

I tell you; we need to meditate and ponder on this scripture until the truth and reality of what it is saying hits home and gets deposited deep within our spirit!

I guarantee it will set you free and empower your faith for all eternity!

It will empower and embolden you, amen!

When you start to realize that the life; the ZOE nature of God is within you; it will set you free!

When you start to realize that the life and nature of God is within you, *that ZOE is within you,* and that it is greater than anything that you can possibly come up against in this world, *you will become unstoppable!*

Listen that ZOE life and nature of God within you, *God Himself within you,* is greater than any contradiction you can possible face that can try and come against your life.

The life and nature of God within you, *God Himself living within you, is greater,*

…He will obliterate every obstacle and every contradiction that comes across your path,

…any attack of the enemy that might come against you, any devil you might face in any circumstance or in any person's life that intersects with your life!

He who is in you is greater, amen!

We have for way too long made way too much of the devil, and of the Fall,

…but God wants us to see that the life and nature of God within us *super-abounds!*

His power within us, through His life, His ZOE, His resurrection life within us,

***supersedes anything and everything amen,
<u>it supersedes everything</u>!***

Where sin and death and darkness abounded,
grace did much more abound,

...it super-abounded in the resurrection,

...and death was swallowed up in life!

*...that resurrection life, the ZOE of God
super-abounded,*

*...and it super-abounds in us today still,
amen!*

**The life and nature of God that is within our
lives, within our very life, *super-abounds*,**

*...it is out of all proportion to the power of
darkness;*

...it abounds super abundantly above!

I tell you, sometimes, in my own times of
worship and praise, ***a boldness comes over
me, and I realize that, through our God, we
shall do valiantly!***

*...In my spirit I become so aware of who I am, I
see myself, that I am seated with Christ in
heavenly places, **that I am seated with Him in
a place of absolute authority.***

…I see myself there as I am simply praising and worshiping my God, *and a boldness comes upon me* **as I am seeing myself in that place, seated at the right hand of my Father God, seated there in Jesus,**

…and as I am in that place worshiping and praising God, **I become aware of the fact that I am treading down the enemy,** *I am treading the enemy under foot.*

I can literally see myself in the spirit realm doing that, even though I am caught up in God, even though I am simply focused on my Father and simply praising and worshiping Him, *and not even thinking about the enemy or giving him any attention whatsoever!*

He is defeated and under our feet, amen!

…and in that place of worship and exalting my Father and my God **a greater and greater boldness comes upon me and begins to grow within me,**

…and I see myself as what He has called me, as what He says I am, and what He has called me to be!

Listen, the glory of God has got to be manifested upon this earth!

It should not just stay in prayer and in our praise and worship; *it is meant to spill over into our very lives, amen!*

144

We have to so align ourselves with God, with that ZOE nature of God and allow it to flow through our being, *allow Him to flow into our very being,*

...so we may yield to Him, and so we may truly come alive, and allow that life, that ZOE life and nature of God, to flow freely, to flow through our lives, from out of our very being,

...so that we can start taking a step of boldness until we walk in that flow and walk in that boldness!

You see, you might be seeing yourself, in prayer and in praise and worship, *you might be seeing yourself put the enemy under your feet,* **laying hands on the sick and driving out sickness and disease,**

*...and you might be doing it **in your spirit,** seeing yourself, imagining yourself doing it,* there in that place of prayer, *in that place of the spirit,*

...but as soon as you go out into the world around you, into the natural dimension, *that vision is going to be challenged,*

...but God wants us to go out with joy and be led forth with peace from out of His presence;

He wants us to leave His presence <u>just as bold</u> as we were a minute ago, when we were before Him.

He wants us to go out and walk in that same mind!

He wants us to go out and walk in that same boldness!

God wants that atmosphere of worship to be cultivated and to continue within you, *within your heart, within your spirit,* <u>to where you don't close down your spirit anymore</u> after a specific time of praise and worship,

...but you continue to feed off of His faithfulness, <u>off of His nearness</u>,

*...and now that specific time set aside may be over, but in the presence of your brethren, and in the presence of the world **your spirit remains awake and open,***

...there is an openness in your spirit and a surrender in your spirit to that LIFE,

...so that that ZOE life and the love of God can continue to flow!

...that love and life of God is continually flowing <u>from you</u> *to them.*

We must learn to feed off of each other's spirit.

We can no longer afford to live our lives with a closed off spirit, *with a shutdown spirit.*

We can no longer afford to close up shop!

'Oh, you know, my Christianity is my own private thing!'

No, no, no!

Listen, you are indebted to humanity!

The life within you, the life you enjoy, that ZOE life makes you indebted to humanity!

Listen, no longer live for yourself!

Begin to take a bold step in your spiritual life!

Begin to step out in ministry to others and start releasing the life of God that's within your spirit!

Start releasing that life and giving it out freely!

Freely you have received, *freely give!*

If you know and can see how to move in the gifts of the Spirit *then start moving in it more and releasing it!*

If you have received some prophecies, *start stepping out and fulfilling those prophecies in your life!*

God is holding you responsible for seeing yourself according to what He has spoken over your life,

...and then to complete and begin to bring to fulfillment those prophesies!

Of course there are prophecies spoken over us, declarations about what God is going to do in our lives, and with us, somewhere in the future, *that only God can make come to pass,*

...but there are many prophecies spoken over believer's lives *that will never ever come to pass* **unless they start laying a hold of eternal life to which they were called.**

Paul said to his spiritual son, Timothy,

1Timothy 1:18-19

"This charge I commit to you, Timothy, my son, in accordance with the prophetic utterances which pointed to you, <u>so that inspired by them you may wage the good warfare</u>,

(*...that warfare has nothing to do with fighting the devil, **but it has everything to do with) holding faith and a good conscience...***"

He goes on to say in chapter 4:14 & 15,

"Do not neglect the gift you have, which was given you by prophetic utterance when the elders laid their hands upon you.

Practice these things; <u>devote yourself to them</u>, so that all may see your progress."

And then in 2Timothy 1:5-14,

"I am reminded (*...and I want to remind you also*) **of your sincere faith,**

...a faith that first dwelt in your grandmother Lois and your mother Eunice, and now, I am sure, dwells in you (still).*"*

"Hence I remind you to rekindle the gift of God that is within you through the laying on of my hands;

...for God did not give us a spirit of timidity, (but of boldness);

...He has given us a spirit of power, and of love, and of self-control, and of a sound mind."

*"**Do not be ashamed then** (or bashful) **about testifying to our Lord, nor of me his prisoner,**

*...**but take your share of suffering for the sake of the gospel, in the power of God, who saved us and called us with a holy calling,**

*...**not in virtue of our works, but in virtue of His own purpose and the grace which He gave us in Christ Jesus ages ago, but now has also manifested, through the appearing of our Savior Christ Jesus, who abolished death, and brought life and immortality to light, through the gospel**."*

Paul says in verse 14,

*"**Guard the truth that has been entrusted to you by the Holy Spirit who dwells within us!**"*

Listen, God is holding each and every one of us responsible **to step out boldly**

God is holding **you** responsible **for stepping out boldly!**

I am reminded of the life of a young eagle, and I am sure we have all seen the documentaries, but for in case you don't know what I am talking about, let me quickly fill you in.

Just like that little eagle grows up and begins to develop feathers and begins to develop its little wings.

It sits there in that nest and the mother has been feeding it and feeding it and feeding it. And there comes a day when it outgrows the nest.

Just like with us, we have been sitting under the divine instruction, under the truth of the gospel and its full implications,

...especially those of us who have been schooled in the word of righteousness, and who accurately understand the message of grace, and did not grow up under some warped teaching on grace,

...and what happens in our spirit is,

...we have been fed the divine word of God, we have been fed the honey from the rock, **and as we are embracing the truth we are growing faster and faster in our understanding and in our revelation of these things, *and that revelation begins to sink in deeper and deeper, until we are overwhelmed with its reality, and we become transformed by it,***

...and as a little eagle, we sit there in the nest, *and we are seeing all these more mature eagles flying over us,*

…and just like those little eaglets, I am sure they can see themselves there, flying with the others, they can see themselves in their minds eye, in their imagination, *they can see themselves among the mature,*

…and as their mother comes to feed them they open their mouths wide open again, *just wanting to be fed, just wanting to grow, just wanting to mature,*

…but when the time comes, when those little eaglets are past ready, *God comes and brings a soberness into that nest, into the relationship between the mother and those little eagles,*

…and the mother stops feeding those little ones, not to starve them, but to get them ready, **to get them out of their comfort zone,**

…*and she starts calling for them, and then starts nudging them, and pulling them out of the nest onto the ledge,*

…*and if they succumb to fear, she starts pulling the feathers out of the nest, so they are left with sticks and thorns* **and it becomes very uncomfortable for them within that next,**

…**and she keeps gently coaxing them and calling them and pulling them out of that comfort zone and challenging them to get on her back and come fly with her.**

Now once she has had them on her back and flying with her for a little while, *then she takes them high up into the sky and she lets go of them and flies out from underneath them **and basically leaves them with no other choice but to fly.***

They have to start flapping their little wings and learn to fly themselves.

She gets them to discover that they too can fly that they too can figure this thing out!

...that they too can learn how to function as an adult eagle and not a little helpless eaglet anymore!

Let me tell you something, just like in the case of the relationship between the mother eagle and the little eaglet, between the adult eagles and their children, **God is faithful, *and He wants us to grow up in all things into Him who is the head of the body, Christ Jesus Himself!***

...into the fullness of the measure of the mature stature of Christ!

Our Father loves us and because of that intense love for us, He knows that we will never get anywhere *unless we come into the fullness of what we were designed for!*

For an eagle, there is no life outside of flying!

If that little eagle resists the mother and refuses to deal with its fears, and the mother cannot get it to co-operate, *that little eagle will either eventually fall off of that cliff, **or die in that nest!***

I am telling you; **God wants us to grow up!**

He knows that **outside of our design, *outside of coming into the fullness of that ZOE life and nature of God, the fullness of the life of the Spirit within us,***

*...**outside of coming into the abundance of life we were designed to live, there is no real LIFE for us as a Christian, there is no real fulfillment, there is no real hope for us!***

God had an adventurous life in the spirit in mind for each and every one of us!

We are indebted to live after the spirit, *outside of that, there is only death.*

God didn't have death in mind for us!

God didn't have a dead life full of dead religious works in mind for us!

No, He had an adventurous life in mind for us!

An abundant life!

Therefore, God will challenge every known comfort zone, *because He is holding us responsible for growing up and becoming His witnesses!*

...to become manifest epistles of Christ, read and known by all men!

...to be letters of recommendation, recommending the Gospel, being ourselves open statements of the truth!

...getting up on a high mountain and lifting up our voices with strength, *giving voice and clarity to the gospel!*

...lighting a lamp *and setting it on a pedestal so that it might give light to everyone in the room,* **to everyone one around us,**

...because we are the light of the world, *a city set on a hill that cannot be hidden!*

We are the leaven *that leavens the whole lump!*

We are the salt of the earth!

I know this is very sobering and very challenging,

...but God wants to sober up each, and every believer, and He wants us to know that we will not fall flat on our face,

...because He is faithful in His love and in His commitment to us!

He will never leave us *nor forsake us!*

He has soaring outside of the nest in mind for us!

And He is saying,

'Trust Me, just trust Me, Confront your fears and trust Me, I have soaring in mind for you, nothing less!

...If you step out I will make you soar!

...And if you stumble I will lift you up and make you soar again!

...I will not leave you nor forsake you!

...Do not be faint of heart,

...be strong and be bold, be very courageous, because I am with you!

...You will not fail; you will succeed because I am with you!

...I will be there for you and lead you into triumph, if you will only trust Me and step out!

...Step out My child, step out of your comfort zone, stretch your wings and fly!'

Listen it really is time to start releasing *what God has placed within our spirit!*

Each and every one of us have received that same quality; *that same quality of life as what Jesus had,*

...that same quality of life than what Jesus *has, amen!*

As He is, *not as He was,* **but as He is** <u>right</u> <u>now</u>, *so are we* <u>*in this world!*</u>   - 1John 4:17

Of His fullness have we all received!

We have received grace beyond measure!

Each and every one of us have received that same quality of life that Jesus has and walked in while here on earth.

I tell you; *He ruled over the laws of nature!*

*...**and God has that same quality of life,** that* *same kind of ruling in mind for us!*

We are seated with Christ, *and the principalities and powers are under our feet,* *they are way beneath us,*

*...**because we are seated far above all rule** **and authority, all power and dominion and** **might, and every other negative force that** **can be named!***

We are seated with Christ, and we are ruling from a heavenly position!

We are ruling over the nations *from out of a heavenly position!*

We are priests and kings unto our God!

We are a holy nation and a royal priesthood, *and we rule with Christ!*

We are co-heirs with Him of the grace of LIFE!

We are the bride of Christ!

We are heirs of God and equal heirs with Christ Jesus, *and we co-reign with Him!*

We share His executive authority with Him!

We are ruling from a heavenly position!

We are ruling over the nations *from a heavenly position!*

We are ruling over them!

We have got to start seeing ourselves like that!

We have got to start seeing ourselves that way!

158

We have got to start seeing the fact of who we are in Christ!

…that we are engrafted in Christ Jesus,

…that, in Him, we live and move,

…walking on the face of this earth as aliens, *as invaders of this natural world!*

Jesus once told His disciples:

"…I am the resurrection and the life, he who BELIEVES in Me, though he were dead, yet shall he live!"

…and then Jesus again came to His disciples after the resurrection and He reminded them of that reality, He said to them, look,

'I was dead and behold I live forevermore!'

Can you just imagine the kind of persuasion that Jesus was speaking from to His disciples?

…and you know what, that is exactly the kind of persuasion from which we speak,

…it is the exact kind of persuasion we move in,

…it is exactly the kind of platform of persuasion from which we work;

…exactly the same!

…because we too **realize that,**

'I have been crucified with Christ Jesus, I have descended with Him into the portals of hell, into the gates of hell, into the very depths of hell, but on the third day, God's resurrection power entered us,

…God's resurrection power entered me, and I have been lifted up, and I stand upon this earth in newness of life!'

You see, to my friends and family it might seem odd,

…I might seem odd now, but I am telling you, that within me **there is something boiling!**

Inside of me there is a release of energy and of the life and nature of God, within my spirit, amen!

Ha… ha… ha…

I am full of the nature of God and of that life and energy, amen!

…and I am releasing it,

…and I am stepping out in boldness, amen!

…and I'm releasing it unto you in this book!

…imparting it to your spirit!

God wants us to release that life inside of us!

God wants us to get bolder, amen!

You see, because we can no longer afford to keep God prisoner in our lives!

We can no longer afford to keep Him imprisoned within our lives!

Chapter 10

Stepping out of your comfort zone

I just want us to take a look at Joshua's life quickly.

In Numbers 13 we are told the story of the 12 spies that were sent into the land, *but how that Joshua and Caleb were **of a different spirit** than the rest.*

When they came back, ten of them came back with a negative report, but Joshua and Caleb came back saying,

*"**We are well able to take the land, because God has given us the land!**"*

*"**He has given us the giants living in the land and ruling over the land as our prey!**"*

*"**We are well able to take the land, because God has given us the land!**"*

*"**We are well able to take that land; we are well able to possess that land in the name of our Lord, because our God is a consuming fire, and we go out and come in***

from that consuming fire, and He goes out before us as a consuming fire!"

The other ten spies they were so sense ruled, they said,

'No, we look like grasshoppers in their sight, we are like grasshoppers!'

...just like proverbs says,

"As a man thinks in his heart so is he!"

"As a man will think so he will be!"

If you want to be a grasshopper, you must stay a grasshopper!

If you are a grasshopper in your thinking, and in your believing about yourself, *you will stay a grasshopper!*

But, *"As a man thinks in his heart so is he!"*

"As a man thinks so he will be!"

...and you've got to start seeing yourself as God sees you!

...and you've got to start releasing the new creation life, that is within your spirit, to your natural life,

...to this natural environment you live in,

...to this natural life that is around you,

*...*so that when people look at your life, when they see the life that surrounds you, *they know that it is a direct reflection of your spirit!*

...because there is no longer a thing of closing up your spirit,

...a thing of shutting down and stopping the flow of your spirit,

...because you know God is holding you responsible to be mature and keep flying, and soaring with Him, and being that eagle you are!

God is holding you responsible to open up those floodgates that are within your spirit *and to keep them open within you,*

*...*and to keep allowing that living water to flow,

*...*that truth, that faith that is within you,

*...*allowing it to keep flowing freely,

*...*that water of life that is within you,

*...*allowing it to gush forth *...*and to torrent over every obstacle that comes into your path and tries to get in your way.

Joshua and Caleb were of a different spirit.

And we see there now in Joshua chapter one that God was speaking to him, and remember, Moses had just died, and now he, Joshua, has got to take over, and God says to him, He says,

Joshua 1:2

"Moses My servant is dead; now therefore I tell YOU, arise, and go over this Jordan, you and all these people, into the land which I am giving them"

Listen, through this passage *God is speaking to us right now!*

God is speaking to you!

…and He says,

Verse 3,

"Every place that the sole of your foot will tread I have given it to you!"

You see as you are sitting there, reading this book, *you are sitting in the reality that <u>you have been freed</u>.*

You have been made free!

I mean <u>we have been freed</u>!

We have been made free!

I have been set free!

...and so have you!

...*and we are so <u>free</u>!*

We can live free in the beautiful revelation and acknowledgment of righteousness,

...*but there are people out there in the world, who legally have exactly what you have,*

...*what we have, what we have all been given in Christ Jesus,*

...*they legally have exactly what we have,*

...*but through ignorance they have been kept in bondage!*

...*so we, you and I, we have got to go and divide to them their inheritance!*

God is holding us responsible; *He is holding you responsible* to no longer be selfish,

...*but to go and divide to them their inheritance!*

...*to divide to them that inheritance which you have already become a partaker of!*

Joshua 1:3

"Every place that the sole of your foot will tread I have given it to you!"

Verse 4,

"...all the land ...towards the going down of the sun shall be your territory!"

...it shall be your pondering ground, amen!

"No man shall be able to stand before you all the days of your life; as I was with Moses, so I will be with you; I will not fail you nor forsake you!"

God is saying that to you, BELIEVER, He is saying it to you!

"...as I was with Moses, I will be with you; I will not fail you nor forsake you!"

Verse 6,

"Therefore, be strong and of good courage; for it is to the people you shall divide an inheritance."

It is to the people out there in the world, still trapped in ignorance *that you and I are going to divide an inheritance to,*

...because God has given us; He has given me, and He has given you *the keys of heaven and hell.*

He has given you and me all authority in heaven and hell to bind whatever you will and to lose whatever you will *and it shall be done in heaven, amen!*

He has given you and me all authority in heaven and hell *to bind whatever you find that needs binding here on earth,*

...and to lose whatever you will in the kingdom, the things of God that needs loosing; *that inheritance that belongs to the people of this world!*

"...it is to the people you shall divide an inheritance, which I swore to their fathers to give them."

"Only be strong and very courageous, being careful to observe and to live by all the things which I had commanded you; turn not from it to the right hand or the left, that you may have good success wherever you go!"

"This book of the law shall not depart from your mouth, but you shall meditate in it day and night, so that you may observe to do according to all that is written; for then you shall make your way prosperous, and then you shall have good success."

"Have I not commanded you, '…to be strong and of good courage?' Do not be afraid, nor be discouraged and downcast; for the Lord God is with you wherever you go!"

So, as we can see from what was written here, *Joshua had to be the man, who would have to rise and stand up,*

…so that he may divide to the people the inheritance that was due them

But God knew that there was no way that Joshua could do it if he was not God minded.

That is why God said to him, *'If you meditate upon My word, day and night,*

*…if you are willing to pay the price that must be paid, **THEN** you will make your way prosperous, and **THEN** you will have good success!'*

Let me tell you, if you want to reach new heights with God, *if you want to start seeing every person and every obstacle and every circumstance in your life through the eyes of God,* you are going to have to get up into that High place,

…you are going to have to come up higher,

...you are going to have to come to that place where you see yourself seated with Christ in heavenly places,

...you are going to have to come to the place of renewing of the mind,

...to the heights of renewing your mind!

...you are going to have to get there!

...you are going to have to get to those heights!

You see; God said to Joshua,

'If you would renew your mind, if you would not let My words depart from your pondering, from your meditation, from your mouth, if you would mutter and speak it to yourself and declare it over yourself, THEN you will get the breakthrough, THEN you will make your way prosperous, and you will have good success!'

As Joshua was actually doing these things, what was happening to him?

What was happening *in his spirit?*

He was becoming intertwined with God's thoughts.

The faith of God was rubbing off on him and being imparted to his spirit!

Faith was being imparted and strengthened in his spirit!

He was being strengthened with might in his inner man, by the Spirit of God!

He was then in a position to divide the inheritance to the people!

He was now in a position to divide to them the spoil!

He had to be strong and very courageous,

...and he became strong and very courageous!

In this passage of Scripture God says 4 times,

'Be strong and of good courage!'

'Only be strong and be very courageous!'

You see, there is a step that you take, when you say, *'Father, I am now stepping out of that mess I am in'*

...and you say,

'Father I am now stepping out of even the slightest thought for my life, I am taking no thought for any kind of security on this earth. I am stepping out of any form of security on this earth; any other foundation

I could be building my life upon and relying upon, other than YOU,'

'...because I realize that this earth realm we live in is unstable and shakable and very shaky. This world we rely on is shaky; it can so easily fall apart and disappoint us again!'

'...because the Scriptures makes it clear that it is easier for heaven and earth itself to pass away than for Your word to pass away or to become unstable and unreliable and shaky!'

You see, it is a place you come to within your spirit, to where you get to the position, to the realization, to where you say,

'Father this earth is too shaky for me!'

'This world is way too shaky for me to rely on any further!'

'*...everything that my eye can see Father, I realize now that it is temporal, and everything that my eyes cannot see **that** is eternal!*'

'*...everything that my eye can see **was created out of that which is not seen**'*

You see, what has to happen is, in our own lives we have got to come to that place where we can say,

'Father, I am taking that step,

…where I am living …I am now living in the spirit,

…I am more at home in the spirit than I am in the natural'

'I am more at home in the spirit realm, in Your Spirit-realm,

…because the things that are spiritual <u>are more of a reality to me</u> than the things which my eyes can see!'

And what is that spiritual realm?

What is that realm I am referring to?

It is that realm of eternal truth!

God's revealed LOGOS truth and creation truth and redemption truth!

It is this truth Jesus referred to when He said:

"And you shall know the truth and the truth shall set you free!"

"…you will know the reality, spirit reality,

…the reality of your original design, of your authentic design,

...you will know the reality of your true spirit identity, redeemed and restored,

...and that truth, <u>that reality</u>, will set you free!"

"...you will know the fact, you will know <u>the reality</u>, that the spiritual realm, that your relationship with Me, <u>is much more sound</u>, a much more sure foundation,

...much more of a foundation than this world you are relying on,

...than even the earth you are standing on!"

"The very seat you are sitting in now and trusting in right now is too shaky, it's too shaky!"

"...but there is a much more sure foundation, much more reliable, and that is the foundation of the spirit; <u>spirit truth, spirit reality</u>!

...<u>eternal spirit truth and spirit reality</u>!"

That foundation of the spirit; that sure foundation, *becomes mine and it becomes yours,*

...it becomes ours when we start walking in the spirit,

...when you start walking conscious of spirit truth and spirit reality and you start walking in it,

...and you start walking with the Spirit, and you start walking with God.

As we are here, in the presence of God, discussing these things together in this book, *my spirit is aware of God,* **and I realize that He is ministering to us,**

...He is ministering to me and He is ministering to you right now as you are reading this book,

...and as we abide in that spirit realm, in that spiritual mentality, in that mentality of being aware of spirit truth, and of the presence of the Holy Spirit Himself,

...and in our conversations also in our day to day living, as we fellowship around these things with each other, *we are caught away, we get ruptured, caught away in our spirit man, into the realm of the Spirit, into that realm of spirit reality, into that reality,*

...we are caught away, and we are embraced by those things, by those truths, by that reality, by the Spirit of God Himself,

...and we are walking in a supernatural reality, in a supernatural dimension, in a Spirit dimension!

...and so we are walking in the supernatural 24 hours a day, hallelujah!

...we are walking in an eternal reality and an eternal realm, amen!

...we have tapped into and are totally connected to eternity, amen!

...we have passed from death to life, and we are enjoying eternal life in the here and now, amen!

...it's called abundant life, amen!

...life in the spirit!

And so, **God is calling us to be strong and courageous!**

And that's the step we all must take to get to that position to where we say,

'Father, I have no more security on the face of the earth; all of my security is in the spirit, all of my security is in that realm, in your truth, all of my security is in the Spirit; in You!'

...we are just like that little eagle,

...we cannot afford to want to cling to the safety of that nest, no, *we've got to jump,*

...we have got to jump,

...we've got to start using those wings,

*...we've got to start soaring on the winds;
we've got to start soaring in the spirit,*

...and God is calling us to rely on His Spirit.

God is calling us to soar in the Spirit, amen!

**You see the will of God for our lives does
not always equate to our comfort in the
flesh.**

**He wants to take us out of our comfort zone
and let us partake of His glory as we soar
with Him in the Spirit and become co-
workers together with Him, *co-laborers in
the work of the ministry,***

**...co-laborers in the advancement of His
influence in people's hearts and lives,
*through His truth and through His love!***

Every time Paul received instruction from the
Holy Spirit *to go to minister in a foreign place,*
**he broke down every closed door, and
every wall of resistance** set up by men who
opposed the truth and love of God, and who
opposed the will of God.

**Paul often stepped out of his comfort zone,
and he stepped out on a limb, and ended up
ministering to others at great personal cost
to himself, *but advancing the truth and love
of God in the process.***

178

"Five times, Paul says, I have received at the hands of the Jews the forty lashes less one.

…Three times I have been beaten with rods;

…once I was stoned.

…Three times I have been shipwrecked;

…a night and a day I have been adrift at sea;

…on frequent journeys,

…in danger from rivers,

…danger from robbers,

…danger from my own people,

…dangers from the Gentiles,

…danger in the city,

…danger in the wilderness,

…danger at sea,

…danger from false brethren;

…in toil and hardship,

…through many a sleepless night,

…in hunger and thirst,

…often without food,

…in cold and exposure,

…and, apart from other things, there is the daily pressure upon me of my passionate concern and burden for all the churches.

…Who is weak, and I am not weak?

…Who is made to fail, and I am not indignant?"
                                        - 2Corinthins 11:24-29

You see, when the truth and love of God and His call upon our lives to share that truth and love comes knocking at the door of our heart, *we are challenged to silence that voice that reminds us of the fleshly comfort zone we may have to sacrifice and of all the fleshly comforts we may have to give up or lose out on having and enjoying.*

Listen that voice is just a distraction that wants to rob you of that adventurous abundant life in God!

That voice is very deceptive and subtle and may come at you from a direction you least expect it!

*I mean, sometimes it comes through loved ones, even through our pastors, and even from other people **we have known and respected and trusted for years.***

Jesus said this in Matthew 10:34-39

"Do not think that I have come to bring peace on earth; I have not come to bring peace, but a sword.

…For I have come to set a man against his father, and a daughter against her mother-in-law; and a man's foes will be those of his own household.

…He who loves father and mother more than Me is not worthy of Me;

…and he who loves son or daughter more than Me is not worthy of Me;

…and he who does not take his cross and follow Me is not worthy of Me.

…He who finds his life (his natural life) will lose it, and he who loses that life for My sake will find it!"

We must learn to silence within ourselves, every doubtful divisive voice that rises up,

… *every thought that exalts itself against the knowledge of God,*

…and we need to boldly address it just like Jesus had to when He said:

"Get behind Me, Satan! For you are not mindful of the things of God, but the things of men" - Mark 8:33

Listen don't go and rebuke your well-meaning family members, or your sweet loving pastor who is trying to look out for your good. *You will just wound them because they do not understand.*

Just say in your heart to God:

"Father, forgive them, they do not know what they are doing!"

Don't judge them and reject them, *but don't you dare listen to those naysayers either!*

Don't listen to that voice of ignorance and unbelief no matter where it comes from,

…and don't allow those people **to smother your faith and put your fire out with a wet blanket!**

Every time the transforming fire of revelation knowledge into the truth and love of God comes into your spirit *your heart will be set ablaze.*

The life and faith of God will be ignited in you all over again, afresh and anew!

There will be a refreshing and renewal in your understanding, and in your thinking, *and your passion will be ignited!*

Clear revelation into God's truth and love sets your heart on fire every time,

...and then it challenges your life and every comfort zone you may be compromising with and settling for!

In Mark Chapter 1, Jesus approached Peter and Andrew about following Him, as they were fishing with their father Zebedee.

It is very interesting to note that Jesus did not ask them,

'Hey, listen guys, is this a good time for you to leave your father's side to run the family business by himself, so that you can come and hang out with Me, and get involved in the work of ministry?'

No,

He did not say,

'As soon as you have at least three confirmations, and five prophetic words, oh, and the all-important approval of your pastor,

*...and only if you really-really want to, **then, come and work with Me in the ministry!***'

No, the call of Jesus interrupted their little program and came and confronted them as they were in the middle of life, mending fishing nets with their dad, taking care of the family business.

The Scriptures indicate that **they jumped at the invitation.**

They did not hesitate and say,

'You know what Jesus; we'll have to get back to you on that!'

No,

They immediately dropped what they were doing, *however important it might have been at the time,* **and they followed Jesus.**

They dropped the family business, the salary, the retirement plan, everything, *just to trust and yield to Jesus and trust in His goodness and to be able to enter into that abundant life He promises.*

It's a faith thing!

It's a trust thing!

It's a love thing!

It's a friendship and love relationship based on trust!

184

They stepped out of their comfort zone; they stepped out in faith, *because they trusted in the love of God,*

...because there was more security in the things of the kingdom, in that spirit-life, than in the life of the flesh!

They disconnected from the voice of human reasoning and logic, doubt and fear, *and they connected with that voice of God that was coming to them in Jesus!*

Hebrews 4:12 says,

"For the word of God is living and active, sharper than any two-edged sword, piercing to the division of soul and spirit,

...and is a discerner of the thoughts and intents of the heart,

...and that discernment no creature can escape,

...but all are laid bare before the eyes of Him with whom we are dealing with (namely God)*."*

You see, the truth of God, that word of God that comes to you by revelation *is a piercing sword and discerner of the thoughts and intents of the heart.*

Sometimes it cuts like a knife, a skilled scalpel full of truth and love, and full of God's power to transform a person into the very image and likeness of Christ;

...that very image and likeness we were designed for,

...that very image and likeness we already are in the spirit, in our inner man, in our spirit!

That scalpel of God's truth and love and revelation comes to cut away everything that does not match up with that nature and life and faith that is within our hearts and our spirit already.

It comes to cut out cancerous attitudes and habits and doubts and fears that are contrary to the Christ-life in us.

It comes to burn those things out of us by the truth and grace and faith and power of God; *by the fire of His love!*

Listen, if we do not allow our heart attitudes and our motives, and our faith, *to be challenged by the scalpel of God's truth and love,* **then how will the fire and passion in our hearts continue to burn?**

...then how will our hearts ever be challenged?

....then how will we ever be challenged to step out in spite of our fears and natural reasoning,

...then how will we ever be challenged to step out in faith and love?

Chapter 11

Be bold and be strong! Fear not!

God is bringing a new boldness into His body, into the Church, **through revelation, through truth and love,**

...a fire and a passion is ignited,

...and it comes alive and challenges us in our inner man to stand up and be strong and to step out in faith and love!

God is igniting that boldness, that sense of faith,

...where I'm acknowledging that faith that is already within me and that is now being awakened and ignited through the incorruptible light and spark of His word;

...through that incorruptible life that is in His word!

...and I'm stepping out into a new boldness and into a new realm of strength and courage, a new realm of faith and life, ZOE life, amen!

What's going to happen **when I step out in faith,** and I say,

'Father, I'm no longer keeping You prisoner in my life, but I'm setting Your life free to bring everything into compliance that comes into its path and gets in its way?'

Isaiah 35:1-2 says,

"The wilderness and the wasteland shall become glad, and the desert shall rejoice and blossom; like the crocus it shall blossom abundantly, and rejoice with joy and singing"

I am telling you, wow, when we start releasing the ZOE nature and life of God within us, *that's exactly what's going to happen!*

"...it shall blossom abundantly and rejoice!"

"Glory shall be given to them and majesty!"

How shall they get it?

Where shall they get it from?

"They shall see the glory of the Lord and the majesty of God!"

They shall see it in us and through us, amen ...**because, you see, the glory of God cannot be seen *until you release it in your life!***

*...**until you take a step of boldness and release it!***

And now Isaiah goes on to say,

Verse 3,

"Therefore, strengthen the weak hands, and make firm the feeble knees. Say to those who are fearful hearted, 'Be strong and do not fear!'"

You see **in the truth of redemption** God comes to you and He says to you,

*'**Be strong and courageous!**'*

Listen through this book, *and through His work of redemption, through His truth and love,* **God is calling you today to take a new step of boldness in your life!**

He is saying,

*'**Come into a new boldness!**'*

God wants His declaration of victory over you to be within you, to be released within your spirit, to where you are walking in it, not just in the congregation and the gathering of the saints, *but also when you are out there in the world and you are walking alone,*

*...**and you are now realizing I am not alone, I do not have to be weak, I can be bold, that***

191

same boldness, that same declaration of victory is in my spirit, and I am releasing it to mankind!

"Behold your God will come with vengeance, He will recompense His enemy, and He will come and save you!"

He says,

Verse 5,

"Then the eyes of the blind shall be opened and they'll see..."

You see; the manifestation of the Spirit can only come *when you release what's in you already!*

It will only happen when you release that life and nature of God within you!

...when that life that ZOE is gushing out of you, out of your spirit,

You see you cannot minister with a closed spirit and expect any kind of manifestation of the Spirit!

No, you have to rip those gates completely off its hinges, *you have to open those floodgates into your spirit and those floodgates out of your spirit,* you have to open them completely and allow the full flow of His Spirit to flow through your life!

*…and you see **only then** will this happen,*

He says, verse 5 to 7,

"Then will the eyes of the blind be opened and they'll see…"

"Then will the ears of the deaf be unstopped,

…and the lame shall leap as a deer.

…The tongue of the dumb shall sing for joy,"

"…and the water shall break forth and have a breakthrough in the desert;

…the burning sand shall become a pool,

…and the dry and scorched, the parched and thirsty ground, shall become springs of water;"

Listen this is not just some vague prophecy, some unlikely thing, *no, listen this is a **reality!***

This is *our reality* in Christ Jesus!

And it is speaking directly to us!

Know this reality!

…because knowing this reality will set you free, amen!

"...and the tongue of the dumb shall sing, and water shall <u>burst forth</u> in the wilderness and <u>streams</u> in the desert; the parched ground shall become a pool, and the thirsty land, <u>springs of water</u>; and in the habitation of the geckos, and the jackals, where each lay, there shall be a marchland of grass with reeds and rushes!"

Hallelujah!

Isaiah 35:8

"...a road shall be there, a highway, and it shall be called 'the highway of holiness' or 'the Holy Way;' the unclean shall not pass over it"

...that means that **no man will be able to come across your path and not be affected by your life!**

...**because your life will be a natural reflection of your spirit, amen!**

...**because you are allowing those streams to flow and affect and water and quench the thirst of humanity!**

Listen we are indebted to do it!

How can we fellowship with so much abundance *and not allow it to flow?*

We owe it to humanity to share the abundance we enjoy!

"...the unclean shall not pass over it, but it shall be for others who walk on the road. Although a fool shall go astray, no lion shall be there, nor shall any ravenous beast go on it, they shall not be found there, but the redeemed shall walk there!"

Verse 10,

"...the ransomed of the Lord shall return (...they shall return home to where they belong upon that highway, and they shall exit the wilderness), *and come to Zion with singing; with everlasting joy within their heads; they shall obtain joy and rejoice with gladness and sorrow and sighing shall flee away!"*

That is the life of every BELIEVER!

...that is the abundant life which Jesus came to offer to everyone who has gone astray and got lost in a wilderness!

Hallelujah!

That is our life!

That is the life we walk in!

That is the life of everyone who has fully embraced and believed their salvation in Jesus!

As we read this passage, **that life that it speaks of is not the life that we hope to have one day,**

...maybe one day when we get to heaven,

...or maybe one day when we're holy enough!

NO! Start recognizing who you are!

Start recognizing what God has placed within your spirit, and put off that inferiority mindset, that inferiority complex!

Rip those gates of ignorance and inferiority off its hinges and start releasing the power and glory and life; the grace of God that is within you,

...and let it begin to flow through you!

Listen, as E. W. Kenyon put it so aptly in one of His many books:

We stand in the presence of lost humanity, in the realization that I have full authority to open the floodgates of heaven and release the grace, the life, and the love of God to that lost humanity as good as dead!

You see, when you stand in the presence of a lost humanity, *and we know that they are, amen,*

...so, when you stand in the presence of a lost humanity, *you stand there with that knowledge,*

...but you also stand there *with the realization that you have full authority to open the floodgates of heaven to them!*

YOU have full authority to open the floodgates of heaven to them, amen!

"...and sorrow and sighing shall flee away!"

Chapter 12

Thousands upon thousands of people depend on us!

Let's go to Isaiah 40, turn with me there in your own Bible, and we'll end our study with that chapter.

If you have to, go read these Scripture passages I have quoted from, in various different translations,

…it just gets more and more beautiful,

…and different things will pop out at you *as you read it phrased differently than you have always heard it or read it.*

This is a major key to making the Scriptures, and your relationship with God **come alive!**

The Holy Spirit will use it to impart the depth, the clarity, and the beauty of what He is communicating in those Scriptures to your spirit!

Listen, in these Scriptures, **we are seeing what the Spirit of God, what the prophetic**

Spirit of Christ in these Scriptures has got to say to us!

Have ears to hear what the Spirit of God and of Christ is saying to us!

Hear what the Spirit of the Lord is saying to you!

In this book and by these Scriptures He is commissioning you!

He is compelling you to start releasing what He has placed within you!

He wants to awaken what is within you, what has always been within you, so you can fully release it, amen!

He imparts the truth to you in order to awaken that dormant seed, that ZOE life and nature of God that lies dormant within you!

Just like the rain and the snow comes down from heaven, and imparts its LIFE to the dormant seed in the desert, in order to awaken the LIFE, to awaken that dormant LIFE that is within that seed, buried within that wilderness, within that desert, just waiting to be awakened, just waiting for the moisture and LIFE of the rain and the dew and the snow, to be imparted to it, so that it might live and bring forth its LIFE, *that LIFE that has always been within it!*

You can go and make a more thorough study of this concept in Isaiah 55.

The whole chapter explains to us how salvation and transformation takes place in the wilderness.

It is all the fruit of the impact of the Word; of the LOGOS, of the logic or truth of God; of the thoughts and intent of God made known to us in the Scriptures and finally revealed in Christ when the Word, when that LOGOS, became flesh!

See, the Holy Spirit wants to impact you with truth, *His eternal truth of who you really are, His eternal truth of what He has already placed within you.*

He wants to commission you!

He wants to compel you to start releasing what He has placed within you!

Otherwise, we are just going to be another generation of people who could not *fully* be the salt of the earth and the light of the world!

...all because we cannot see our worth,

...and therefore the world cannot see our value either, and the value of what we have to give them, and we are trampled underfoot by the world!

We cannot afford to allow another future generation to fulfill these prophecies *as if they do not belong to us!*

Listen, in my own life I cannot allow that, *I could not bear the thought!*

Listen, we are fulfilling the prophecies, *and we are the fulfillment of Scripture, amen!*

We are that people Isaiah wrote and prophesied about!

We are the planting of the Lord!

We are the redeemed of the Lord!

We are mount Zion, the city of the Lord!

A city set on a hill that cannot be hidden, amen!

We are partakers of the divine nature!

We are the light of the world!

As He is so are we in this world!

We are the offspring and children of the Lord!

We are the ones who cry, ABBA Father, DADDY God!

We are the sons of God!

The whole earth is groaning, in labor pains, until this very day it is crying out. *Humanity is desperate and crying out for the full manifestation of the sons of God!*

It is high time for us to believe that we are who God says we are!

We are whom the world is crying out for!

We have their deliverance in our mouth and in our hands!

Salvation has come!

Salvation is here!

We are the fulfillment of all the prophecies; we are the fulfillment of Scripture!

In our very midst, they are coming to completion!

"Unless the grain of wheat falls into the ground and dies, it remains alone, but if it dies..."

...and it died, amen,

...Jesus already died, amen,

"...but if it dies, it produces much grain!"
- John 12:24

...after its own quality and kind, amen!

...the grain of wheat that is the fruit that is produced, matches the grain of wheat that fell into the ground and died!

Hallelujah!

Glory to God!

We are the fruit of the travail of His soul!

We are the fruit of the travail that satisfied His soul!

We are the satisfaction of God!

We are the fulfillment of His hopes and dreams!

We are complete in Christ Jesus!
– Colossians 2:10

We are His workmanship completed in Christ Jesus! - Ephesians 2:10

We are walking and acting in the realm of the new creation!

...in the realm of a quickened and activated spirit!

We are walking and living in that realm!

God is commissioning you here Zion!

Isaiah 40:1-2

"Comfort, yes I speak comfort to you My people, says your God. Speak tenderly to Jerusalem, speak comfort to her, and cry out to her that <u>her warfare is ended</u>..."

What warfare?

That warfare against sin!

That warfare against principalities and powers!

They [the principalities and powers; the enemy and his forces, the forces of ignorance and of darkness and spiritual blindness] *are now trying to wrestle us off of our stand!*

...They are now desperately trying to wrestle against our faith!

...But they are weak against that faith!

...They are no match for our faith!

...This is the victory that overcomes the world; that overcomes them; that overcomes anything and everything, *even our faith,*

...the very faith of God we have embraced;

...the faith that has once and for all been delivered to the saints!

They [the principalities and powers; the enemy and his forces, the forces of ignorance and of darkness and spiritual blindness] *are hopelessly trying to undo the truth in our minds* **which we have come to understand and embrace!**

They are warring against us, **but we are not at war!**

We are resting!

We are seated!

We are seated with Christ, enjoying Him!

We are not warring with them over anything!

We don't have to argue with the devil over anything!

We are not fighting with him in prayer even!

There is no fight!

We don't have to fight darkness; *with the truth we dispel it!*

With authority we cast it out!

We undo its stronghold in people's minds!

We are no longer caught up in a war against the flesh,

...nor against the forces of darkness!

We are more than conquerors!

The enemy and all his forces have been defeated!

Jesus' victory is fully ours, NOW!

It is *fully* ours!

The only possible power the enemy has is the power of ignorance and unbelief!

That is the only power he has left,

...and it is not a power in and of itself,

...it is merely the absence of truth and faith!

The enemy only flourishes in an environment of confusion!

He only functions in an environment of half-truths, and of lies and deception and doubt and unbelief!

But we know the truth, the whole truth, and that truth sets us free and keeps us free!

We don't have to fear or fight with or wrestle the enemy anymore!

The Spirit of God says prophetically through Isaiah to us,

"Comfort, yes speak comfort to My people, says your God. Speak tenderly to Jerusalem, speak comfort to her, and cry out to her that <u>her warfare is ended</u>..."

"...say to her that her iniquity is pardoned, and that she has received from the Lord's hand double (pardon) for all her sins!"

This whole world is still caught up in warfare *with a defeated foe.*

They are caught up in a war with sin!

They are caught up in a mindset of, *"The good I want to do I cannot do. The things I desire to do, the things that are right and proper, I do not find the strength to do! The things I do not want to do, those things that are wrong and shameful, evil even, those things I do not want to do, within me there is something compelling me to do them!"*

That is the warfare that is going on within the religious ignorant church, and within the world right now, today,

...but we have got to lift up our voice with strength and release to them this revelation which God is revealing and imparting and placing within our spirit right now, amen!

(I wrote more about this topic of freedom from sin in my book: *"Resurrection Life Now!"*)

Isaiah 40:2

"...cry out to her that her warfare is ended, say to her that her iniquity <u>is pardoned</u>, and that she has received from the Lord's hand double (pardon) for all her sins!"

"You are the voice of one crying in the wilderness!

Prepare the way (the road, the highway) **of the Lord!**

Make straight into the wilderness a highway for our God!"

Through Christ, through the work of redemption, through the truth revealed, he says,

Verse 4,

"Every valley shall be lifted up, end every mountain and hill be made low; the uneven ground shall become level, and the rough places a plain,"

...**the rough places, the ground in people's hearts and minds shall be made smooth,**

...**that means, every obstacle shall be removed, every lie and every deception, every thought that exalts itself against the knowledge of God shall be arrested as if by spear point;**

…it shall be dealt with and straightened out!

…it shall be accurately addressed and removed by the sharp two edged word, by the scalpel of God's truth revealed in Christ and then restored in redemption and proclaimed in the gospel we preach!

Verse 5 makes it plain,

"The glory of the Lord shall be revealed!"

Hallelujah!

The glory of the Lord shall be revealed *through your life!*

Through YOUR life!

Through the LIFE you have to enjoy!

Through the truth upon your lips, amen!

"The glory of the Lord shall be revealed, and all flesh shall see it together, for the mouth of the Lord has spoken!"

Verse 6 to 8,

"A voice says, 'Cry out!'"

I looked up those words *"cry out"* and it means to preach or proclaim, pronounce and publish, teach, reveal through teaching, speaking truth through an utterance.

...it implies speaking aloud with excitement, as in with boldness and confidence, enthusiastic and joyous about the truth of the matter!

I am telling you now; God is commissioning us to open our mouths and to start speaking forth what God has placed within our spirit, amen!

Isaiah goes on to say,

"A voice says, 'Cry out!' And I said, 'What shall I cry?"

"Cry aloud, 'All flesh is as grass, and all its loveliness is like the flower of the field. The grass withers, and the flower fades, BUT ONLY UNTIL the breath of the Lord (the breath of life) *blows upon it!"*

"Surely the people are as grass. The grass withers and the flower fades; BUT the word of the Lord (the truth of God, that word of LIFE, that breath of life that our God blows upon us through the gospel, through the word of a successful redemption accomplished in Christ Jesus, that word, that truth of our God) *will stand forever!"*

Verse 9,

"Therefore, get you up to a high mountain O ZION, herald of good tidings; lift up your voice with strength, O Jerusalem, (we are the new Jerusalem, amen, where God dwells by His Spirit. We are that New Jerusalem come down from Heaven, and He says of us that we are the) *herald of good tidings,"*

He says,

"Lift up your voice, lift it up, fear not!"

"Say to the cities of Judah (Judah means, **praise.** He is referring to those who hear and embrace the gospel with gladness; those who accurately esteem or price the truth of the gospel and praise God for it) …*say to the cities of Judah, 'Behold your God!'"*

Isaiah goes on to say,

Verse 10,

"Behold the Lord God comes with might (in the work of redemption, in the gospel) *and His arm rules for Him"*

Jesus is the arm of the Lord revealed.

His right hand has brought for Himself deliverance and salvation.

Jesus is the right hand of God and the arm of the Lord revealed,

...and now we are that arm extended!

We are seated with Him at the right hand of God.

We are the hand of God's authority and rule!

We rule and reign with Him!

We are the arm of the Lord revealed!

"Behold the Lord God comes with might and His arm rules with Him, for Him!"

He says,

"Behold, His reward is with Him!"

...and as we go out preaching the gospel,

"Behold, our reward is with us!"

"Behold the Lord God comes with might, and His arm rules for Him;

...behold, His reward is with Him, and His recompense before Him"

...His vengeance upon His enemies and His recompense of reward upon mankind goes before Him, as we go out before Him!

...we are sent out before His face, and His vengeance upon His enemies and His recompense of reward for mankind to enjoy rests upon us,

...and it comes upon them, as we go out, we bring it to them, amen!

Verse 11 says,

"He will feed His flock like a shepherd, He will gather the lambs in His arms, (through us, amen, through us proclaiming and making plain the gospel to them, amen,) *He will carry them in His bosom, and gently lead those that are with young"*

Ha... ha... ha...

...that is us, amen, pregnant in our spirit with truth,

...pregnant with new disciples, amen, with young believers,

...we carry them within us, within our hearts, within our spirit,

...that desire for evangelism and for discipleship, for preaching the gospel to them and discipeling them in the truth of the gospel.

All we want to see is the impact of the truth upon their hearts and lives as they embrace the gospel.

We carry all that inside us.

There is a compelling within our spirit, a compelling of love, the birthing of new life!

The bursting forth of streams of water!

We carry them within our bosom; we carry the young!

We are pregnant with their salvation; we carry their new life within our spirit, that ZOE life, the life and nature of God that was meant for them,

...the very LIFE of God that is within the gospel and that is within us, and which gives birth to them!

"He will feed His flock like a shepherd, He will gather the lambs in His arms, and He will carry them in His bosom,"

"...and gently lead those that are with young"

Listen, building a highway into a wilderness, into a desert **is not easy going!**

It is not a cake-walk!

Listen, it takes diligence to lay a hold of eternal life to which we are called.

It takes studying to show ourselves approved …a worker that need not be ashamed, *rightly dividing the word of truth!*

It means we have to thoroughly study and understand the gospel,

…*and become fluent in our communication of it!*

We have to proclaim it accurately *in order for it to become effective!*

We cannot be slothful and lazy about it!

Listen; there are thousands upon thousands of people depending upon us, *depending upon our perseverance in the truth!*

…*our perseverance in ascending the mountain of God!*

…our perseverance in grasping and in laying a hold of everything that Jesus Christ has laid a hold of us for in ministry!

…there are thousands upon thousands of souls *depending upon our perseverance in living and proclaiming the truth of the gospel!*

…*they are depending on us to lay a hold of that eternal life to which we are called!*

...they are depending on us to lay a hold of a consistent walk of innocence before God and intimacy in His presence!

...they are depending on us to be anointed, to be and stay full of the anointing, to be able to release that anointing unto them in their time of need!

...that anointing only flows out of a place of intimacy with God, walking in our righteousness,

...embracing that gift of righteousness and reigning in life because of that righteousness!

...living and abiding and flowing out of that place of oneness with our Father, oneness with our God!

...oneness with Jesus, oneness with His Spirit!

Listen, you cannot expect to walk in power, to walk in the anointing of the Holy Spirit, *if you are not walking in harmony with God,*

...walking in harmony with the truth, walking in absolute harmony with your righteousness, walking in harmony with the gospel, walking in total harmony with Jesus, with the Spirit of Truth, with the Spirit of God Himself!

(I have written more about this in my two books about *"Reigning in Righteousness,"* you are welcome to get them and read them as well!)

There are thousands upon thousands of souls that depend on you walking with God!

They are depending on your perseverance in the things of God!

They are depending upon your perseverance in the truth!

They are depending upon the breath of the Lord!

They need the breath of the Lord!

What is the breath of the Lord?

It is the truth of the gospel; it is the word that proceeds from His mouth,

...but you see it is not just a stale old word, it is not just a doctrine,

...it is the fresh word, the word of revelation, the word that is directly proceeding from His mouth,

...it is that word that you receive from Him, that is imparted to you in private, in your heart, in your time with Him, as you fellowship with Him around the truth of the gospel in the privacy of your own heart!

What is the breath of the Lord?

It is the truth of the gospel, but it is not just the truth of the gospel, *it is the anointing!*

It is the anointed truth of the gospel!

The anointing is the ZOE, the very life and presence of the Holy Spirit of God that flows from out of your spirit, out of your inner most being,

...from out of your intimate union with the Father, as you abide in Him, and Him in you

...as you abide in that intimate place of fellowship with Him!

That anointing, that power of God, that life of God, flows out of us and gets imparted to them, through our being,

...it gets imparted in our words, and as we lay our hands upon the sick and release what we have inside of us!

The anointing which abides in us; which we have from the Holy One *is tangible and transferable!*

We impart it to them,

...and it sets them free!

But I want you to know and understand that the anointing is not just a power,

…the anointing is not just an *'it;'* an invisible force of some sort.

Because God abides in us, in our spirit, and we abide in Him, in relationship with Him in our spirit, *the anointing is the very presence and life of God Himself,*

…the very Spirit of God Himself!

God Himself combines Spirit with spirit as we speak the truth of the gospel!

Jesus said:

"My words are Spirit and life!"

God imparts Himself, His very life, His very power, His very Spirit, His very presence,

…God imparts Himself through our words,

…and through the laying on of our hands!

The very Spirit of God is imparted to people, *and He sets them free!*

Hallelujah!

The whole New Testament, beginning in the gospels and all the way through, is full of examples of how the anointing and presence and Spirit of God is tangible and transferable and can be imparted to someone else!

After making a study of it, you can then go and look in the Old Covenant Scriptures and find the same thing there!

You see; you are the vehicle and the instrument and the mouth piece that God is going to use in people's lives,

...to impart His ZOE to them, to impart His very life and power and Spirit, to impart Himself to them!

Unless the breath of the Lord moves upon them and blows upon them *through you,* they will just be as another generation of grass!

Now in its natural season, in the season of grass, in that natural dimension, the grass produced the best flower that it could, *but it began to fade, it had to fade, it fades, it has no other choice but to fade, and it fades,*

...BUT when the breath of the Lord blows upon it, and breathes life into it, it will stand and it will last forever!

...it will have a glory which stretches to everlasting, amen!

"All flesh is as grass, and all its loveliness is like the flower of the field. The grass withers and the flower fades, UNLESS the breath of the Lord blows upon it!"

"Surely the people are as grass. The grass withers and the flower fades; BUT the word of our God stays forever!"

"O ZION, you who have received good tidings, you get up into the high mountain…"

…start walking in that presence of God that is your portion, 24 hours a day.

God is not far from any one of us.

He is near unto us.

He is within your reach.

He is within you even!

That intimate relationship is within your reach.

You cannot get any closer than being one Spirit with Him,

…but you've got to start walking in that dimension,

...you've got to start tuning in and tapping into that nearness, into that very presence of God that is within you, within your spirit!

God sustains all life!

Your Father, His presence, His person, He Himself is as near to you as your next breath!

Listen, you are in the presence of God *right now!*

You have to locate Him *in your spirit;*

...you have to find Him there,

*...*not in outer space somewhere!

You are connected to the ZOE!

You are already connected to the supernatural!

You already are a spirit being!

You will never be more of a spirit than you already are!

Therefore, make up your mind, you are either connected to the ZOE or you are connected to the SUKEY!

You are who you are!

You are more connected to the ZOE than you are to the SUKEY!

I am who I am in His presence!

I am who I am!

I can either flow in the supernatural or be stuck in the SUKEY;

I can either flow in the ZOE or live a mere natural existence!

I am either in the ZOE, or I'm not!

Listen, you are in the ZOE!

You are connected to the supernatural dimension of the Spirit of God!

You are connected to the spirit realm!

You are connected to the Spirit of God!

You are connected to that dimension of life;

...you gain access through faith into that dimension, into that grace in which we already stand!

Listen, to those who grasp these things in your spirit, *the supernatural are going to be natural!*

divine intervention is going to be a common everyday occurrence to you!

…not that it would be common,

…but that supernatural dimension would be a familiar, comfortable thing, easy to access and flow in,

…like you were designed for it, because you were, amen!

The very breath of heaven that we live in, the very breath you breathe *is supernatural,*

…because within it is the very creative force and nature and power of God!

"O ZION, you who have received good tidings, and bring good tidings, get up into the high mountain and lift up your voice with strength, with boldness and with confidence,

…O Jerusalem (the dwelling place of God), lift up your voice and be not afraid, say to the cities of Judah, to the people created for His praise, say to them, 'Behold your God!'…"

Why do we have to say to them, *'Behold your God!'?*

Because they were not beholding their God,

...because they were not mindful of Him, but they were instead living a SUKEY minded life!

But you see, the moment they lift up their eyes and behold their God *they are changed and transformed instantly into His likeness!*

Just like a caterpillar who is transformed into a butterfly, and he sheds that old skin, that old life of a caterpillar, because the caterpillar really always has been and always will be a butterfly, not a caterpillar!

Listen you are a butterfly, not a caterpillar!

You have always been a butterfly, even though you have lived the life of a caterpillar!

The moment you behold God, what happens?

The things of this earth grow strangely dim in the light of His beauty, *in the light of His glory and grace revealed unto you!*

The things of this earth *grow strangely dim!*

As you behold your God *you are transformed and conformed into His image, into His likeness,*

...you are no longer fashioned after this world, conformed according to its SUKAY mindset, its natural minded thinking,

...you are no longer fashioned after that natural image,

...but you are conformed, you are transformed into God's image and likeness!

"...say to the cities of Judah; say to the people created for His praise, 'Behold your God!'..."

Isaiah 40:27 says,

"Why do you say, o Jacob, (Jacob means rebellious one, or deceived one who deceives others),

...Why do you say, o Jacob, and speak, O Israel, (Israel means prince of God, or son of God, *but you see the sons of God are deceived,* so He says,)

...Why do you say O Israel, 'My way is hidden from the Lord, and my right is disregarded by my God!'?

Listen, have you not known?

Have you not heard?

The Lord is the everlasting God, the Creator of the ends of the earth!

He does not faint or grow weary,"

You see, in the SUKEY *there will always be a fainting and weariness!*

There will always be weakness, and tiredness and weariness,

…but when you feel that weakness, *you get rid of it in Jesus name,* **because we are walking in the reality of resurrection power,**

…we are walking in the reality of newness of life!

…we are walking in the reality of our unbroken connection with ZOE life, the life and nature and power of God;

…we are directly connected to His sustaining life-force!

Isaiah 40:28 & 29 goes on to say,

"God neither faints nor is weary. There is no searching in His understanding. He gives power to the weak, and to those who have no might, He increases strength…"

Who are those who have no might and power?

It is those who are living in the SUKEY, *those who are living the normal span and course of a human life.*

…They will grow weary. Why?

Because they fail to intertwine with Him!

They fail to intertwine with God!

Verse 30,

*"**Even the youth shall faint and be weary, and the young men shall utterly fall, exhausted…**"*

You see; that's the glory of the flesh; the young men are the glory of the flesh.

The young men in their prime, in their strength, that is their glory.

The young women in their youthful beauty, which is their glory, *but it is going to fade,*

…they are going to fade *unless they intertwine with the living God,*

…*unless they start intertwining with the ZOE nature and life of God!*

*"**Even the youth shall faint and be weary, and the young men shall utterly fall, exhausted;**"*

*"**But those who wait upon the Lord** (QAVAH in the Hebrew …those who intertwine with the Lord, becoming one with Him,* **they shall draw upon His strength; *His strength becomes***

229

theirs, they enter into a relational strength **to where He imparts His strength to them,**)

…they shall renew their strength,

…they shall mount up with wings as eagles,

…they shall run and not be weary,

…they shall walk and not faint."

You see, what is happening now?

My normal span of my human life, my season here on planet earth, *I have now intertwined it with God. I am now intertwined with the ZOE life of God!*

When I run I am not weary, when I walk I do not faint!

But instead, I mount up with wings as eagles do.

*…I mount up, and I soar **because it is no longer I that live, but it is Christ Jesus that is alive within me!***

That little Hebrew word *'QAVAH'* makes all the difference in the world!

It is the picture of *a relational strength …of a symbiotic relationship,* where say for instance, a morning glory, which is a type of a flowering vine, winds itself around a sturdy tree trunk.

You see; the morning glory is a tender vine type plant that has no strength to hold itself up off the ground, and to reach for the sun in a wooded area,

…but it uses the strength of the tree to climb and wraps itself around the tree, **intertwining with its strength.**

That word *'QAVAH'* also gives the picture of *an inter-relational strength.*

If you take for instance something like fiberglass and you pour it into a weaker plastic container, *that fiberglass takes on the outer appearance of that plastic container;*

…it takes on the softness, and the texture, the very weakness of that plastic container,

*…**but that plastic container takes on the enduring strength of that fiberglass within it.***

You see, and that is exactly what has happened with us; *we are intertwined with the ZOE nature of God, through the impartation of faith, through the impartation of the Spirit of God, through the impartation and embrace that came to us through the gospel.*

Listen we are not ordinary people anymore!

We are not mere men!

We are embraced of God!

We are invaders of the sense-realm!

And now for the rest of our lives, every day of our lives we want to plunder every form of darkness!

…and if it does not simply come across our path, because maybe they are running in the opposite direction, *we go out and we chase after it, we go, and we chase after them and we invade their space and their privacy with the good news so that we may undo the works of darkness in their lives, amen!*

Hallelujah!

We are responsible for releasing that ZOE life that is within our spirit, *because we are not mere men,*

…even though we may walk on this earth *resembling mere men,* **we are not mere men anymore,**

…**we are ambassadors of this new life, this ZOE life of God that has come into the earth,**

…*and we represent that life, that ZOE,*

…*we represent its invasion and takeover of this planet!*

Hallelujah!

We represent the establishing of a whole new life!

...the life of the Spirit!

ZOE LIFE!

If we want to be the salt of the earth, the light of the world; if we want to shine as lights in the midst of a crooked and perverse generation, *then we have got to start releasing the power and the glory and the grace of God through our lives,*

...and through every word that we speak!

And all this comes through that intertwining!

When I intertwine with God, when I intertwine with the Spirit of God, when I intertwine with the ZOE life of God, with the anointing of God, *then I run and I am not weary, I walk and I do not faint!*

When I intertwine with Jesus, then I mount up with wings, I lift up my wings, and I fly like an eagle and I soar and I get up into higher heights now, *I get up into the heights of heaven where I belong, and there is a new boldness now within my spirit,*

...and I can lift up my voice with confidence and with strength, because I am not ashamed of the gospel of God,

...for I know it is the truth, and I know now it is the power of God, and I intimately know that power,

...and I know that the gospel is the power of God and has the power to save every human being and every human life on the face of this earth!

Father, I just thank you that this word has fallen on the inclined ears of BELIEVERS!

I thank you that every word that is spoken, Father, has fallen into fertile ground, ground that embraces your seed, your life-seed, your ZOE life!

And Father, I thank you that You by Your Spirit bring about the growth of this word,

...You bring about the pondering and the musing and the meditation, and the thoughts about this, within the hearts of every BELIEVER,

...and each and every reader, Father!

I thank you for quickening a meditation and a thinking upon these things within each and every reader, Father,

…that they might take hold of the truth of this word, *because this word written down does not mean they are walking in it,* **but there has got to come a taking hold of it from within,**

…*from within their own hearts, so that it might be lived out in their own lives!*

Father, I thank you that we can make these things our own,

…and that by Your Spirit, my God, You quicken within each of us that desire and that hunger and that passion to lay a hold of that which is ours in Christ Jesus, and of that for which Christ Jesus has laid a hold of us for!

I thank you Father that from that laying ahold there will also then come an effective sharing of faith, *an effective sharing,*

…and a full acknowledgement of what is ours in Christ Jesus, *of what is in us,* **of what is in us already!**

And I thank you, Father, **for the explosion of outreach, the evangelism explosion that will come from the impact of this book upon the hearts and spiritual ears of the BELIEVERS.**

I thank you Father *that we are not of this earth,*

…but we are invading it through personal evangelism and programmed outreach, and

whatever form of sharing our faith may take on my God!

Thank you Father *for the reality of walking in the supernatural,*

…that we will walk in the supernatural signs and wonders of the Holy Spirit, of the anointing that You have placed within us,

…and that we no longer have to try and strive for it and try and earn it,

…but we walk in it by faith,

…we lay a hold of it in prayer and in intertwining with you, **because that is our destiny!**

Thank you for Your exceedingly great and precious promises towards us,

…and that they are no longer mere promises, *mere empty promises, or just set aside for a select few to obtain and walk in,*

…but You have said, Jesus, *that the same works You do and greater,* **we shall do also!**

I thank you that the very fact that we are ZOE manifested on SUKEY ground *is supernatural already my God!*

We are one with the supernatural!

We are one with the Spirit of God!

We are one with God!

We are one with You already, Father God, *and therefore we expect the supernatural,*

…when we go out and when we step out to minister to someone, *we step out in high expectation, my God,*

…because we are one with Your ZOE life, with your power, with your anointing,

*…and we thank you that **that anointing is tangible and transferable,***

*…**and it will be imparted by You Spirit within us as we minister to people, Father!***

Father, we thank you for Spirit-impact upon people's lives *as we minister to them your word,*

*…**and as we lay hands upon the sick!***

We thank you that **You confirm your word with signs and wonders,** Father,

…and that *we are merely co-workers together with You,* **but it is You who bring the impartation and the impact and the growth within people, Father!**

We thank you **for Spirit-impact** as we minister, *because people will see the light, they will see a great light;* **they will see the light of Your Glory and grace in our words and even upon our faces as we behold You and as we witness for You!**

We thank you Father that **we are what we are by Your grace, Father God!**

Thank you that we can behold You Father God!

And we thank you that **You are who you are!**

You are what You have revealed yourself to be in Christ Jesus, in Your grace!

We are who we are, *and there is no boasting in the flesh my God,*

*…**but there is only an absolute reliance and dependence upon You!***

There is only an intertwining with You, *for without You we can do nothing, and without You we are nothing,*

*…**but within You we live and move and have our being, Father God!***

Thank you for that intertwining of our spirit with Your Spirit Father God,

...thank you for that intertwining with You, for that total intertwining with You,

...that absolute intertwining of our spirits,

...and that fullness we enjoy because of it!

You are our exceedingly great reward, Father God!

...and we are your delight!

We are yours, exclusively, Father!

Thank you that we have come to fullness of life in You!

Thank you that Your word to us is:

You are My faithful upon the earth!

My very face upon the earth!

My excellent ones!

My glory!

In you is all of My delight!

Amen

In closing, I urge you to get yourself a copy of *"The Mirror Bible"* available online at: www.friendsofthemirror.com or at www.amazon.com and several other book sellers.

If you want me or someone a part of our team to come to where you are, *anywhere in the world,* and give a talk or teach you and some of your friends *about the gospel message and these redemption realities,* simply contact us at www.livingwordintl.com *…*or you can always find me on www.facebook.com

If your life has changed as a result of reading this book, *please write to me and let me know.*

I would love to share your joy *…so that my joy in writing this book may be full!*

"That which was from the beginning,

which we have heard
(with our spiritual ears),
which we have seen
(with our spiritual eyes),
which we have looked upon
(beheld, focused our attention upon),
and which our hands have also handled
(which we have also experienced),

concerning the Word of life,
we declare to you,

that you also may have this
fellowship with us;

and truly our fellowship is
with the Father
and with His Son Jesus Christ.

And these things we write to you
that your joy may be full."

- 1John 1:1-4

About the Author

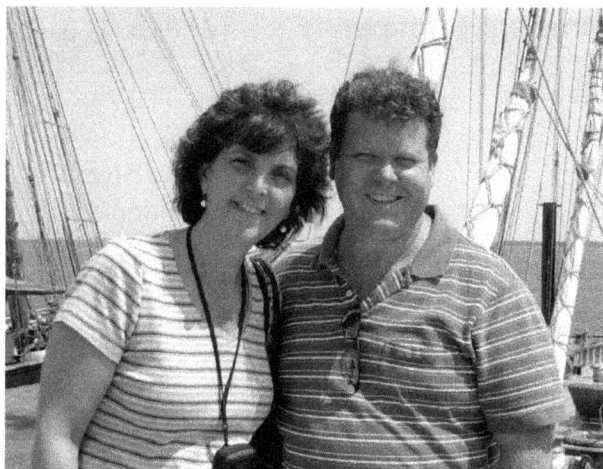

Rudi & Carmen Louw together oversee and pastor a church: Living Word International.

They also travel and minister both locally and internationally.

Rudi was born and raised in the country of South Africa, while Carmen grew up in Cortland, New York.

They function in the ministry of reconciliation (2Corinthians 5:18-21) and flow strongly in the gifts of the Holy Spirit and His anointing to teach, preach, prophecy, heal and whatever is needed to touch people's lives with the reality of God's love and power.

God has given them keen insight into what He has to say to mankind in the work of redemption, concerning the revelation of, and restoration of, **humanity's true identity,**

…and therefore they emphasize THE GOSPEL; IN CHRIST REALITIES; the GRACE of God; the WORD OF RIGHTEOUSNESS *and all such eternal truths essential to salvation and living of the CHRIST-LIFE.*

They have been granted this wisdom and revelation into the knowledge of God by the resurrected Spirit of Jesus Christ, *to establish and strengthen believers in the faith of God, and to activate them in ministering to others.*

Not only are people set free from the poison and bondage of sin, condemnation and all kinds of intimidation, (upheld, strengthened and reinforced by age old religious ideas born out of ignorance,) but many are brought into a closer more intimate relationship with Father God, as Daddy, through accurate teaching, and unveiling of the gospel message, prophetic words, healings and miracles.

Rudi & Carmen are closely knitted together with many other effective Christians, church fellowships, and groups of believers who share the same revelation and passion.